PAYING W(

IN A

HOMESCHOOL

ORGANIZATION

CAROL TOPP, CPA

AMBASSADOR PUBLISHING
CINCINNATI, OHIO

Paying Workers in a Homeschool Organization —2nd ed.
ISBN 978-0-9909579-3-5

Ambassador Publishing
Cincinnati, OH
www.HomeschoolCPA.com.com Carol@HomeschoolCPA.com

Book Layout ©2013 BookDesignTemplates.com
Author photo: Sarah Topp

Disclaimer and Limitation of Liability

This book is designed to provide accurate and authoritative information about the subject matter covered. The author is not rending legal, accounting, or other profes-sional advice.

The fact that a company, organization or website is mentioned does not mean that the author endorses the information or services provided. The resources mentioned in this book should be evaluated by the reader. Readers should also be aware that organiza-tions and web sites mentioned may have been changed or ceased operations since the publication of this book.

Every effort has been made to contact cited quotes for permission of use.

TABLE OF CONTENTS

Dedication

Thank you to all the homeschool leaders who have served their members so generously and taught me so much. I admire you immensely.

Thank you to my beta readers for your comments, suggestions and questions. I appreciate your time and honesty.

Carol Topp

Chapter 1: Can You Pay a Volunteer?

Homeschooling is growing and becoming more popular every year. As homeschooling grows, so do homeschool organizations, co-ops, and groups. Some homeschool organizations get so large that they can no longer be run solely by volunteers. It is not uncommon to find a homeschool group hiring teachers to run a class or paying other workers. This book discusses paying workers in a homeschool organization. Before I discuss hiring paid workers in the following chapters, let's start by discussing paying volunteers.

CAN YOU PAY A VOLUNTEER?

Most homeschool leaders put in many hours a week, all unpaid. That is the definition of volunteer—they are not paid. As soon as a volunteer is paid, he or she is no longer a volunteer. She is (probably) an employee. But I hear from many homeschool leaders who email me asking,

"Can we pay our homeschool co-op director? She works so hard."

Yes, your homeschool organization can pay someone who works for the organization, but the pay must be reported to the Internal Revenue Service (IRS). The reporting responsibility will be on both the homeschool organization and the worker. Additionally, the organization will have to determine if the worker is an employee or an independent contractor. Other chapters in this book cover the required reporting and worker classification.

Many homeschool organizations, especially small or all-volunteer organizations, avoid paying workers. Instead of paying a worker, they show appreciation in a variety of ways such as:

- Reduced fees or tuition. Reduced tuition for classes or for a homeschool co-op fee is a nontaxable fringe benefit if it is *insignificant* (more on that later). If the tuition reduction is significant, the value of the tuition is taxable income to the volunteer.
- Gift cards, but they could be taxable income to the recipient if the cards are a replacement for payment for services and not a true gift.
- Non-cash gifts such as flowers, books, a coffee mug or chocolate are excellent ways to express appreciation and are tax-free to the volunteer.

I'll discuss each of these types of compensation (reduced fees, gift cards and non-cash gifts) to a volunteer in detail.

Tuition Discounts to Volunteers

Schools, private schools, and homeschooling co-ops frequently offer tuition discounts or a reduction in fees to parents who volunteer. If a parent volunteers to teach a class at a homeschool co-op a few hours a week and receives a tuition reduction for this commitment, it could be considered taxable income to the parent.

Whether the tuition discount is taxable income depends on several factors. But let's start first with how the Internal Revenue Service (IRS) defines compensation and especially taxable compensation.

What is Taxable Compensation?

In general, the IRS broadly interprets compensation. It is more than just wages paid. Taxable compensation can include free or reduced tuition given to a parent for his or her service to a homeschool organization.

A worker is no longer a volunteer if he receives something of value in exchange for his service. Therefore, free or reduced tuition given to a parent in exchange for his service would constitute taxable compensation.

From IRS Publication 3079 which, although its title is "Tax-exempt Organizations and Gaming," has a helpful section titled, "Volunteer Labor." The publication states:

> Compensation is interpreted broadly. A worker who obtains goods or services at a reduced price in return for his services may be considered to be compensated.

Then they provide an example:

> ABC Organization operates a private school and sponsors gaming to raise revenue for the school. Parents who work at the gaming session are given a tuition reduction of $50 for each week they work. This reduction of tuition is compensation to the parents; they are not working as "volunteers."

This means that volunteers in a homeschool organization, who get a discount on tuition, would have to report and pay taxes on this "compensation."

But, as with all IRS documents, it pays to keep reading. Publication 3079 also says this:

> On the other hand, a worker who receives *merely insignificant monetary or non-monetary benefits* is considered a volunteer, not a compensated worker. (Emphasis added.)

So if a homeschool organization gives an *insignificant* monetary benefit to its volunteers, it is *not* taxable income. That's good news: **insignificant compensation is not taxable income**! Then, how does the IRS define *insignificant*?

What is Insignificant Compensation?

The IRS does not define insignificant compensation. They only explain:

> Determining whether a benefit is insignificant requires consideration not only of the value of the benefit but also:
>
> • The quantity and quality of the work performed;
> • The cost to the organization of providing the benefit; and
> • The connection between the benefit received and the performance of services.

So the IRS looks at:

- The value of the benefit. The higher the value, the more likely it is significant and therefore taxable income to the recipient.
- The amount and quality of the work performed. The more hours the volunteer works, the more likely that his or her benefit is taxable compensation.
- The cost to the organization. If the cost to the organization to provide a benefit is minimal, the more likely the compensation is insignificant.

- The connection between the benefit and the service. If the benefit is closely tied to the service the volunteers provide, such as an hourly rate, the more likely the compensation will be considered taxable income.

That definition is not very specific, so here are two examples that might help.

INSIGNIFICANT BENEFITS TO A VOLUNTEER

A volunteer teacher in a homeschool program was given a $50 discount off of her $250 tuition for teaching a class. She put in a minimum of 30 hours preparing and teaching this semester-long class. That amounts to an hourly rate of less than $2/hour. So the value of the benefit is low. It costs nothing for the co-op to offer this benefit. The co-op offered this discount as an incentive to increase volunteerism, and it was not taxable income to the volunteer.

If the homeschool co-op offered a full discount of $250 to the teacher, the co-op and the teacher may have to reconsider the taxability of the benefit, since the dollar amount is more significant.

SIGNIFICANT BENEFITS ARE TAXABLE INCOME

Another co-op gave their director several thousands of dollars in gift cards to grocery stores and Target; gave her children free tuition worth $1,500; waived all field trip fees, theater ticket fees, and registration fees amounting to hundreds of dollars in benefits. These benefits were not insignificant and are taxable compensation for her services. The co-op thought that by giving gift cards and reduced tuition they could avoid payroll taxes and the paperwork of hiring and paying their director as an employee. They were wrong! The director should be treated as an employee. She should report all these benefits as taxable compensation.

Homeschool leaders should determine whether the benefits of reduced tuition or fees they are giving to volunteers are insignificant. Look to the IRS guidelines in IRS Publication 3079 listed above. If the benefits are significant and are compensation for services, then the compensation needs to be reported as taxable income to the worker/volunteer.

GIFT CARDS IN LIEU OF CASH OR DISCOUNTS

Some homeschool organizations try to avoid giving cash or tuition discounts as compensation for volunteer service to avoid giving taxable income to their volunteers (and to avoid the required tax reporting the organization must submit). They mistakenly think that gift cards will not be considered taxable compensation. Unfortunately, they are not correct. Often gift cards are given as gifts—small tokens of appreciation. I will discuss gifts later, but here I am referring to significant compensation for services given in the form of gift cards.

The IRS clearly states that gift cards are taxable income.

> Gift certificates that are redeemable for general merchandise or have a cash equivalent value are not de minimis benefits and are taxable.[1]

Let me explain that term *de minimis* benefit. It means a small benefit, so small that accounting for it would be "unreasonable or administratively impracticable." Some benefits like snacks, a coffee mug, a book, etc., are so small that they are a *de minimis* fringe benefit and not taxable income. But the IRS says that cash can never be a *de minimis* benefit since it is not "unreasonable or administratively impracticable" to account for its value. The same applies to cash equivalents, such as gift coupons and certificates. Gift cards, like cash, are never considered a *de minimis* benefit.

The cash and gift cards an organization provides to volunteers do not qualify as *de minimis* fringe benefits, and so they constitute a taxable benefit. However, since the volunteers are not employees, the organization is not required to report the amount of these gifts on a W-2 form. Additionally, a Form 1099-MISC would not be required either if a volunteer receives compensation of $600 or less during the year.

An organization may give small, **non-cash** gifts such as a turkey, book, or a coffee cup without any tax consequences to the recipient because they are insignificant in value and are given as thank-you gifts in appreciation for volunteering.

When is Cash or a Gift Card a Tax-Free Gift?

Gina, a volunteer co-op director, told me this story:

> I was handed an envelope at our last day of co-op, and it contained $75 in small bills. The cash was collected from all the families in the co-op. I did not expect to be paid. I considered this a gift from the families. Do I need to report this as compensation and therefore taxable income?

In order to answer Gina's question, I had to determine if the cash was a gift or compensation for her services and then if the payment was taxable or tax-free. The Internal Revenue Service defines a gift as:

> You make a gift if you give property (including money), or the use of or income from property, without expecting to receive something of at least equal value in return.[2]

The difficulty in determining if payment to a worker is a gift or compensation is that you need to determine the intent of the donor. The IRS has a very difficult time determining intent or expectations. We, on the other hand, can usually determine if a payment is a gift because we know the donor and his or her expectations. The gift of

$75 to the co-op director fits the definition of a gift because it was given to her without any expectation that the families would receive anything in return. That is evidenced by the fact that it came at the end of the co-op year, when there was no expectation of anything in return from the co-op director.

The general rule from the IRS is that any gift is a taxable gift. However, there are many exceptions to this rule. The following are <u>not</u> taxable gifts:

- Gifts that do not exceed the annual exclusion for the calendar year, (for 2016 that threshold is $14,000 per donee, meaning you can give up to $14,000 to a person without triggering a gift tax)
- Tuition or medical expenses you pay directly to a medical or educational institution for someone,
- Gifts to your spouse,
- Gifts to a political organization for its use, and
- Gifts to charities.[3]

The $75 cash gift to Gina the co-op director (the donee) is below the $14,000 threshold, so it is a tax free gift to her.

Be very careful about giving gifts so regularly or frequently that they become expected. One co-op teacher said, "I'm a volunteer, but the year-end gift a teacher received last year was $250, so I expect to get that this year." There should never be an expectation that a gift is coming. Nor should a teacher expect a gift in lieu of compensation.

Examples of Compensation to a Volunteer

Melissa Minimum helps out at her homeschool co-op on occasion, and the board decides to waive her registration fee valued at $35. This fee reduction is insignificant because the value is small and costs the co-op nothing. The $35 is a *de minimis* nontaxable benefit to Melissa.

Vicky Volunteer served as her homeschool co-op's treasurer. The board decides to compensate her in these ways:

- Flowers: a *de minimis* benefit and not taxable
- A book: a *de minimis* benefit and not taxable
- A gift card worth $50 is taxable income
- Tuition discount worth $400 is taxable income.

The total amount of taxable income to Vicky is $450 (the gift card and the tuition discount). Because Vicky is a volunteer and not an employee, she will not receive a W-2. Because the total taxable compensation is less than $600 in the year, the homeschool co-op will not issue Vicky a 1099-MISC either. Vicky should still report the income on her tax return (probably as Other Income on Line 21 of the Form 1040).

Sally Super-volunteer really goes above and beyond in serving as her co-op's president. The board decides to compensate her in these ways:

- Flowers and chocolate are a *de minimis* benefit and not taxable.
- Tickets to the state homeschool convention are non-taxable to Sally since it enhances her skills as a volunteer. In other words, the tickets to a homeschool convention are not for Sally's personal pleasure; they are for the benefit of the organization to have trained and motivated volunteers.
- A gift card worth $100 is taxable income.
- Tuition discount worth $625 is taxable income.

The total amount of taxable income to Sally is $725. The homeschool co-op will issue Sally a W-2, reporting $725 as wages. Since Sally is the board president, she is an officer of the organization. By law, officers of a nonprofit who are compensated are employees. See Chapter: 2 Paying Board Members for details. Sally will report the income on her tax return on Line 7 Wages as an employee. In reality, Sally is not a volunteer, is a compensated board member.

GUIDELINES TO FOLLOW WITH VOLUNTEERS

Homeschool organizations should keep the following guidelines in mind when giving gifts or compensation to their volunteers:

- If an organization gives its volunteers a gift such as food, a coffee cup, a gift basket, book or other item of nominal value, the gift will _not_ be treated as either wages or taxable income to the recipient.

- Although "nominal value"' is not defined anywhere, some tax experts recommend that nonprofit organizations limit the value of noncash gifts to $25.00 per person per year. Twenty-five dollars per person per year is the limit on business expense deductions for gifts that businesses give to their customers or clients.

- Avoid giving cash or gift cards as compensation. If your organization does give cash, check, or a gift card, then explain to the recipient that the amount needs to be reported as taxable income.

- Individuals may offer gifts to your homeschool volunteers in a spontaneous display of appreciation (such as the $75 in cash given to Gina, the co-op director), but an organization that gives gift cards or cash appears to look more like taxable compensation and not a true gift. As one CPA said to me, "A gift comes from your grandmother; an organization gives you taxable compensation." While his rule of thumb is not said that way by the IRS, it's a sensible rule to follow.

- Keep track of the total amount of compensation, including reduced tuition or fee waivers, you are giving to volunteers. You need to give them a W-2 or a 1099MISC to report the taxable income. And by the way, if they are compensated, they are no longer volunteers. They are employees or independent contractors.

THE BEST WAY TO THANK A VOLUNTEERS

- Give small, non-cash gifts such as a fruit basket, cookies, candy, mugs, etc., with a minimal value. Keep it to $25 or less per recipient per year to be on the safe side.
- Pay their way to a homeschool convention with the understanding that this is for the benefit of the organization, not just for the volunteer's personal benefit.
- Host an appreciation dinner for all the volunteers. The IRS states that group meals are a non-taxable fringe benefit.
- Provide coffee, snacks, soft drinks, etc. My co-op had a table of treats set aside only for use by the volunteer teachers (i.e. not for the children!).
- If you want to allow a collection to be taken from your members to give teacher gifts, let it originate from the members and not from your board. Avoid all appearances that this is compensation for services being given by your organization. Let the members collect and award the gift.

My book, *Homeschool Co-ops: How to Start Them, Run Them and Not Burn Out* has a chapter devoted to managing volunteers. The book is available at HomeschoolCPA.com/Bookstore.

FAQ ON VOLUNTEERS

Q: The moms in our co-op do not get paid in money for teaching but are offered "credits" against tuition. Is this allowed?

A: In all likelihood, these "credits" are probably *significant* by the IRS's definition. They are valuable, the amount and quality of the service (teaching) is good, and the benefit is closely tied to the service (the more you teach, the larger the credit). It's allowable to offer your teaching moms these tuition credits, but the value of these credits is taxable income to the parents.

Q: We have one parent who volunteers so much, she doesn't owe any tuition. We actually owe her! What should we do?

A: Some people are what I call "super volunteers." They volunteer so much beyond their discounts or credits that the organization pays them for their extra volunteering. The super volunteer's total compensation is the sum of her tuition credits *and* the extra money she is paid. For example, if her tuition discounts total $1,000 and she is also paid an additional $250 in cash for her services, then her total taxable income is $1,250. She should be given either a 1099-MISC or a W-2 showing total taxable compensation of $1,250. And she is no longer a volunteer.

Q: Our organization provides gifts to several volunteers each year at Christmas. Volunteers receive either a turkey, fruit basket, or gift certificate to a local grocery or department store. The amount of these gifts varies depending on the position, but the range is $20 to $250. Are these gifts taxable to the recipients? How do we report the gifts we give to volunteers?

A: The turkeys and fruit baskets that your organization provides to volunteers are nontaxable *de minimis* fringe benefits that do not need to be reported as taxable income by the volunteers.

The cash and gift certificates that you give to volunteers do not qualify as *de minimis* fringe benefits and they are a taxable benefit. However, since the volunteers are not employees, your organization is not required to report the amount of these gifts on a W-2 form. No Form 1099-MISC is required either, because the volunteers do not receive compensation of $600 or more during the year[4] (the largest gift card is $250). The recipient should report the gift card compensation on her income tax return, but your organization does not have to report the gifts.

Q: My homeschool group is a 501(c)(3) tax-exempt organization. Do these IRS rules still apply to us?

A: Yes, the rules about taxable compensation and reporting apply to *all* organizations, non-profit and for-profit. 501(c)(3) tax-exempt status gives your organization exemption from paying federal income tax on your profit, but it does not give your organization tax exemption for the rules on compensation.

Q: My homeschool group's Board of Directors recently took up a collection from our members as a way of presenting me (their director) with an end-of-year gift of appreciation. The Board collected donations from individual members and then wrote me a check on the group account. This was a complete surprise to me, especially when they presented me with a check totaling over $700!

I'm unsure of how to deal with this tax-wise. The gift was given with the intent of paying my expenses for our state's homeschool convention, including the leadership conference. If I returned the check and used the group's debit card to pay my hotel expenses, would this alleviate the taxes?

A: It sounds as if the co-op was collecting money to defray the expense of sending you to a homeschool convention. It is taxable income to you, because there is an expectation that you will "earn" it by going to the convention (and learning a lot!). If you use the payment on co-op related expenses (like the convention), then you could claim those expenses on your tax return. At the end of the year you should report the $700 as income on your tax return and then report expenses like the convention fee, mileage and hotel costs as deductions. You may break even or show a small profit.

In retrospect, it would have been better if the board had collected the monies and then gave you a nice note saying that you are going to the convention and used the co-op's debit card to pay the expenses. These expenses would not be considered taxable income to you since the money never came to you. And the convention is to develop your leadership skills, not for your personal pleasure (although you may enjoy it!).

Chapter 2: Paying Board Members and Other Leaders

In Chapter 1 I discussed paying volunteers in your homeschool organization. Some of your most devoted volunteers are your board members. Board members of a homeschool groups are hard-working people. They not only homeschool their own children, but they organize support groups and co-ops to help other homeschool families. Sometimes a homeschool group would like to reward these generous individuals, but paying board members presents a unique challenge.

Is It Allowable to Compensate Board Members?

The short answer is yes; a nonprofit homeschool organization can pay its board members. The longer answer is that while allowable, it is very complex and not typical for nonprofit board members to be paid for their service on the board.

A homeschool co-op in the Midwest contacted me recently to apply for 501(c)(3) tax-exempt status. (To learn more about tax-exempt status for your homeschool organization read *The IRS and Your Homeschool Organization* listed in Chapter 9 Resources) The treasurer told me that her co-op had been paying their leaders anywhere from $200 to $1,200 a year for their service on the board. I discussed why paying board members was not a typical practice. Here is what I told them:

- Paying board members can call into question the duty of loyalty of the board member. A board member of a nonprofit has a duty of loyalty to the organization. That means in her role as board member, she puts the organization first in her loyalty. Is she acting in the best interest of the group rather than a personal, financial interest?

- Payments to board members can create a conflict of interest. Is the leader influenced by her personal financial gain or is she considering the best interests of the group?

- Payment could compromise the leader's duty of care. A leader should act in good faith, with the care an ordinary, prudent person would exercise and with the best interest of the group in mind.

- Payments on nonprofit boards is not a typical practice. Charities do not usually compensate their board members. Their funds usually go back into the program. Board members serve because they have a passion for the mission and a concern for the members.

- Board payments can undermine the volunteer spirit of other members. Why should a member volunteer her time when others are paid for their efforts?

- Paying board members can cause dissension and a sense of injustice or imbalance in the group.

- Payments to board members should have member approval. In this particular case, the board voted themselves compensation, but they never put the idea to a member vote. Nonprofit boards cannot vote themselves compensation.

This group wisely decided to stop payments to board members. I think the group will be better served by an all-volunteer board and healthier in the long run.

What Counts as Compensation?

Here is the IRS definition of compensation:

> compensation includes salary or wages, deferred compensation, retirement benefits..., fringe benefits (personal vehicle, meals, lodging, personal *and family educational benefits*, low interest loans, payment of personal travel, entertainment, or other expenses, athletic or country club membership, and personal use of your property), and bonuses.[5] (Emphasis added.)

In another IRS document titled "Reasonable Compensation," the IRS defines compensation as:

1) salary or wages;
2) contributions to pension and profit sharing plans;
3) unpaid deferred compensation;
4) payment of personal expenses;
5) rents, royalties, or fees;
6) personal use of organization's property or facilities.[6]

Regarding number 4, payment of personal expenses—such as education expenses of the board members' children—is taxable compensation.

The IRS does not impose a dollar threshold for taxable fringe benefits. **If your homeschool pays any amount of wages, educational benefits, or personal expenses to board members, it is taxable compensation.**

COMPENSATION TO BOARD MEMBERS IS TAXABLE INCOME

I recently reviewed the bylaws for a homeschool organization that stated,

> Members of the Board of Directors may receive reasonable compensation for their services and may be reimbursed for actual expenses incurred in the maintenance of their duties.

A homeschool organization can compensate their board for their service, but **compensation to board members is taxable income.** If the board member is an officer (chair, vice chair, secretary, or treasurer) he or she must be paid as *employees*. Other board members who are not officers can be paid as independent contractors and given a Form 1099-MISC. See Chapter 5: Tax Forms for Independent Contractors and Chapter 7: Tax Forms for Employers.

Did you catch that? If officers are compensated, the IRS laws[7] say they must be paid as *employees*. That means creating paychecks, paying payroll taxes (Social Security and Medicare), preparing W-2s and quarterly filings with the IRS and your state, and may mean unemployment and workers compensation taxes too! Take a look at Chapter 6: Payroll Taxes for Employers and Chapter 7: Tax Forms for Employers to see what is involved in paying employees.

Does your homeschool group really want to deal with payroll? It can become an excessive burden on a treasurer or expensive if your organization hires a bookkeeper or payroll service. If you do choose to compensate your board members, I highly recommend using a payroll service. See Chapter 9: Resources for a list of payroll services.

EXAMPLE OF A BOARD VOTING ITSELF COMPENSATION

Here's an example that might bring this into reality. A homeschool co-op is run by all volunteers. As the co-op grew, the responsibilities of the five board members grew, too. The treasurer complained that she was spending 10-15 hours every week managing the funds, bills, payments, etc. The president found she was spending that amount of time as well managing volunteers, setting policies, and dealing with problems. They decided they deserved to be paid for their efforts. They had money to do it, so they voted that each of them would receive $500 a semester for their work on the board. It wasn't much considering all the time they put in. To make it easy on the treasurer, they kept their compensation under $600 because they had read somewhere that if payment was under $600 they didn't have to report it to the IRS.

There are problems at so many levels in this example. I wish I could say it was completely fiction, but it is all too true! First, the board cannot vote itself a salary. That's a clear conflict of interest. Additionally, the board giving itself compensation is what the IRS calls private inurement (meaning the revenues of the organization go to the benefit of individuals, especially "insiders" or leaders). Any amount of private inurement can cause a nonprofit to lose its tax-exempt status. *It's that serious.*

But beyond the conflict of interest and private inurement, the board incorrectly thought that this was tax-free money. Keeping compensation under $600 a year simply means that the employer (the homeschool organization in this case) doesn't have to give the worker a Form 1099-MISC at the end of the year. See Chapter 5: Tax Forms for Independent Contractors for more information. But that compensation is still to be reported on the individual's income tax return (probably as Other Income), even if no Form 1099-MISC was issued.

Instead, the board should have put a vote to the membership. The bylaws may need to be amended to allow for a membership vote on board compensation. Or the board could have appointed an independent compensation committee to determine their wages. The board members receiving compensation can have no vote on the amount of compensation. They should not even be in the room when it is discussed. A good Conflict of Interest policy should be created and followed. You can find sample Conflict of Interest policies at HomeschoolCPA.com/Samples. The board should set up a payroll system to pay the officers as employees and the other board members as independent contractors. Or better yet, the board should not seek compensation at all. A bookkeeper could be hired to do some of the work the treasurer is doing. The president should create policies or appoint other board members to handle day-to-day problems, so she is not carrying the burden alone.

REIMBURSEMENT OF EXPENSES

Many times a board member pays for goods or services out of his or her own pocket and then asks to be reimbursed. Reimbursement of expenses is not taxable income if under an accountable plan. An accountable plan requires accounting for the expenses within a reasonable period of time usually by showing a receipt. It does not have to be reported as income to the IRS. Additionally, reimbursement of expenses (if properly accounted for with receipts) should not be included in income reports such as a W-2 or 1099-MISC. For more information on accountable plans, see IRS Publication 535 Chapter 11 and my book *Money Management in a Homeschool Organization* available at HomeschoolCPA.com/Bookstore. .

CAN A BOARD BE GIVEN A DISCOUNT ON FEES?

As I explained in Chapter One on paying volunteers, discounts, if significant are considered taxable compensation to board members. If the discount is insignificant, it is not taxable compensation to a volunteer board member.

Here's some guidance from the Center for Association Leadership (a nonprofit consulting organization):

It is *not* illegal for a nonprofit to compensate its board members with reasonable fees unless prohibited by the organization's bylaws. If compensation is authorized, it is advised that compensation amounts be set by independent directors or an independent compensation committee with input from outside advisors. It needs to be clear that compensation does not imply monetary profit. It is very important that board compensation be comparable to that of other nonprofit organizations and not deemed excessive by the IRS.[8]

HOW CAN WE THANK OUR BOARD?

- Non-cash, small gifts such as food, flowers, a book, etc.
- Giving a small discount on fees.
- Have the organization pay for meals during board meetings.
- Notes and words of appreciation, especially public acknowledgement.
- Priority in class registration.
- Pay for them to attend your state homeschool convention. This may seem like a significant benefit because it can cost the organization quite a bit of money, but it lacks the IRS criteria of a connection between the benefit received and the performance of services. Therefore, paying for your board to attend a conference at the end of the year would not be taxable compensation.
- Plan and pay for a board retreat.
- Buy resources to make their jobs easier including helpful books, hiring a payroll company (your treasurer will love it!), accounting software, etc.

GOOD PRACTICES

Healthy nonprofits have some common practices. Here are a few good practices for your board to put into place regarding compensating board members. For additional good practices regarding financial management read my book *Money Management in a Homeschool Organization.*

Have and use a Conflict of Interest policy. A conflict of interest arises when a board member might receive some personal benefit as a result of a decision the board makes. For example, a board member owns a graphic design business, and the board wishes to hire a graphic designer. This could cause a conflict of interest. A policy should require the board member to recuse herself, which means stepping back and avoiding taking part in the decision-making. Most Conflict of Interest policies ask the affected board member to leave the room and not have a vote on the decision. You can find sample Conflict of Interest policies on my website at HomeschoolCPA.com/Samples.

Establish a compensation committee. This committee should be composed of persons unrelated to the compensated board members and will set the wages and benefits for board members. They will be given guidelines by the treasurer of the total amount available to spend on board compensation, but make the decision on the amount of compensation by themselves. The compensation committee should conduct research into comparable salaries and benefits paid to board members of similar-sized organizations.

Keep your fee waivers to board members small and "insignificant." While the IRS does not define "insignificant," they offer guidelines that I shared in Chapter 1. Have the amount of fee waivers decided by a separate, independent committee or put it to the vote of the full membership. *The board should not vote themselves a fee waiver.*

Add a provision to your bylaws allowing a fee waiver (or tuition discount) to board members or other volunteers. Consider granting a percentage discount instead of a dollar amount. It is recommended that this change to the bylaws be approved by the full membership, not just the board, since the board cannot vote themselves a fee waiver.

FAQ on Compensating Board Members

Q: We don't have a board. We have a leadership team. Do these rules still apply?

A: The IRS uses the common phrase "Board of Directors" to include officer, director, trustee or any individual who has similar powers or responsibilities. So calling your leaders something different from what the IRS calls them does not give your organization a free pass to ignore these tax laws.

Q: Can a member of the board of our homeschool group be given free tuition as a perk? Or could this be a conflict of interest?

A: It is a conflict of interest if the board votes itself tuition discounts. A nonprofit board member has a duty of loyalty to the organization above herself. So if a board votes themselves a tuition discount, their loyalty comes into conflict with their personal benefit.

If only one member receives a discount, the rest of the board could vote to give that person a discount in appreciation for her volunteer efforts. That member benefiting should not be in the room during the discussion on discounts and she should not be allowed a vote.

If the entire board wants a discount for each member, then perhaps the bylaws should state that. If the bylaws are amended, I'd recommend a vote be put to the membership at large approving the discounts as a "perk" of serving on the board.

And remember that unless the free tuition is insignificant, it is taxable income to the board member. I recommend a conflict of interest policy. See samples at HomeschoolCPA.com/Samples/

Q: My homeschool group gives a fee waiver of our dues to our board officers. Would that discount be reported to our officers as taxable compensation?

A: If the fee waiver is insignificant (by the IRS definition mentioned earlier), then the amount is not taxable income. When determining if the fee waiver is significant, consider the following: the value of the benefit, the amount of work the board members perform, the cost to the organization, and the connection between the benefit and the service.

Q: My friend who teaches at a private school gets a 50% discount on her child's tuition and my brother who is a college professor gets free tuition for his kids. Why can't my homeschool group offer discounts on our tuition to our teachers or leaders?

A: You can offer tuition discounts, but they are not tax-free. Only employees of "qualified educational organizations" can receive tax-free tuition reduction for the education of themselves or certain relatives.[9] To be a qualified educational organization a group must:

1. Maintain a regular faculty,
2. Maintain a curriculum, and
3. Have regularly enrolled students.

Qualified educational organizations include institutions such as primary, secondary, preparatory or high schools, and colleges and universities. Homeschool organizations do not meet the definition of a "qualified educational organization" because the IRS goes on to define regular faculty as "qualified" including state certified or trained to be a teacher. Most homeschool groups do not have this standard for their teachers, and if your group does meet these criteria you actually are behaving like a school. Remember that reduced tuition and fees can be offered to your teachers, as long as it is handled and reported as taxable compensation.

Q: Our board members are also teachers in our homeschool co-op. Is that allowed? Can they be paid for teaching and not for board service?

A: Yes. Make it clear in your teacher agreement that the individual is being paid for his or her teaching services and not for service on the board. As a board member, the individual has a conflict of interest when teacher compensation is discussed by the board. This teacher-board member should recuse herself, leave the meeting, and not have a vote regarding teacher compensation.

Chapter 3: Employee or Independent Contractor? Worker Classification

Many homeschool organizations that hire teachers will pay them as independent contractors. Most homeschool groups are nonprofits or small businesses without accounting staff and do not want to deal with the paperwork of paying employment taxes, creating W-2s, etc. The tax paperwork involved in hiring an independent contractor is less complex than the taxes and paperwork for hiring an employee, but the IRS reminds us that the facts and circumstances of the relationship determine worker status, not the organization's preference.

RULE OF THUMB

This chapter goes into a lot of details on the factors you need to consider in classifying a worker in your homeschool organization as an employee or as an independent contractor. But I want to start out with a rule of thumb and then you can dive into the details, keeping in mind your specific organization.

Your organization's right of supervision and control over the worker is the critical issue. Many of the other factors covered in this chapter are tools to uncover evidence of control or lack of control. Always focus your attention on the control factor.

Start by determining whether the worker will be integrated into your organization's operations. If the worker is *not* integrated into your operations and the right of control is not obviously apparent (no training, no work hours, no reports), you are reasonably safe to classify him or her as independent contractors as long as the relationship is short-term.

This would be the scenario if you hired me or another CPA for some consultation or accounting work. I am not integrated into your operations. You will not supervise or control me. Our relationship will be short. I am an independent contractor.

Another example might be a homeschool co-op that hires one or two people from outside the co-op to teach a specific class, but the majority of the teaching is done by volunteers. Although the outside teacher may be slightly integrated into your activities, you can avoid overtly controlling him and have more confidence that he is an independent contractors.

If the worker is integrated into your operations, then your group is at risk of misclassifying him as an independent contractor when he really is an employee, unless several factors point strongly in the direction of independent contractor status. Look for evidence that the worker is truly independent from your organization. Avoid any overt expressions of control. This may mean you have to change some of your practices and policies.

This may be the scenario if all or a significant portion of your homeschool group's teachers are hired (and not volunteers). They are certainly integrated into your homeschool program; without them there would be no homeschool program! There is probably sufficient evidence that your organization is exerting enough control that they should be classified as employees. You may need to either drastically change your behavior and program or read Chapter 6 on how to set up a payroll system for your homeschool organization.

An additional example would be a homeschool program executive director. She is responsible for the daily operations of the program and, therefore, closely integrated into the operations of the program. The board has the right to control and supervise the director. I would venture to say that almost all executive directors of homeschool organizations are employees and not independent contractors.

The decision of independent contractor or employee status is not cut-and-dry. It usually involves a continuum. Your goal is to avoid obvious misclassifications and narrow the area of uncertainty. I know that homeschool organizations may be reluctant to classify workers as employees, but you may conclude that classifying your workers as employees is not that bad, not that expensive, and it lets you sleep at night!

How to Determine Worker Status

Having the proper worker classification is necessary in dealing with several government agencies, including the IRS, the US Department of Labor, and the individual states. To explain how this works, let's start with considering the IRS perspective.

The IRS has a brochure titled *Independent Contractor or Employee* (Publication 1779) to help organizations determine worker status at www.irs.gov/pub/irs-pdf/p1779.pdf.

The IRS uses three factors to determine worker classification:

- Behavioral Control,
- Financial Control, and the
- Type of Relationship itself.

BEHAVIORAL CONTROL

Behavioral control covers whether the business (your homeschool organization) has a right to direct or control how the work is done. This could be through giving instructions or training. In other words, an independent contractor needs no instructions or training to do her job; she already knows how to do her job. When my homeschool co-op hired an art teacher, we looked for someone with an art background. We interviewed several possible workers and discussed what we wanted in an art teacher, but we did not tell her how to run a class or teach art. We exercised no behavioral control since the hired art teacher was an independent contractor.

The following description of behavioral control is from the IRS website:[10]

> Behavioral control refers to facts that show whether there is a right to direct or control how the worker does the work. A worker is an employee when the business has the right to direct and control the worker. The business does not have to actually direct or control the way the work is done – as long as the employer has the right to direct and control the work.
>
> The behavioral control factors fall into the categories of:
> * Type of instructions given
> * Degree of instruction
> * Evaluation systems
> * Training
>
> **Types of Instructions Given**
>
> An employee is generally subject to the business's instructions about when, where, and how to work. All of the following are examples of types of instructions about how to do work.
>
> * When and where to do the work.
> * What tools or equipment to use.
> * What workers to hire or to assist with the work.

- Where to purchase supplies and services.
- What work must be performed by a specified individual.
- What order or sequence to follow when performing the work.

If a homeschool group hires a teacher, they can certainly show her around the co-op, show her to her room, give her the parent policy guide, etc. because all these things help the teacher to perform her task. The co-op should not tell the contract teacher how to conduct her class, what should go into her lesson plans, or where to buy her supplies or get copies made.

Degree of Instruction

Degree of Instruction means that the more detailed the instructions, the more control the business exercises over the worker. More detailed instructions indicate that the worker is an employee. Less detailed instructions reflects less control, indicating that the worker is more likely an independent contractor.

Note: The amount of instruction needed varies among different jobs. Even if no instructions are given, sufficient behavioral control may exist if the employer has the right to control how the work results are achieved. A business may lack the knowledge to instruct some highly specialized professionals; in other cases, the task may require little or no instruction. The key consideration is whether the business has retained the right to control the details of a worker's performance or instead has given up that right.

Evaluation System

If an evaluation system measures the details of how the work is performed, then these factors would point to an employee.

If the evaluation system measures just the end result, then this can point to either an independent contractor or an employee.[11]

You may fear that this evaluation provision means you cannot sit in on the contract teacher's class to watch her teach or conduct a parent satisfaction survey. I think it would be allowable to watch an independent contractor teach. After all, you have the safety and education of the children as your responsibility. Additionally, you want to determine if you will hire her back, so conducting a survey of parents or students is allowed. You might be stepping over the line if you have job performance requirements such as goals, accomplishments, or performance criteria that is used by employers for determining salary. Try to avoid a face-to-face performance evaluation with an independent contractor. Stick to evaluating only the end result: did they teach the class that you hired them to teach?

Training

If the business provides the worker with training on how to do the job, this indicates that the business wants the job done in a particular way. This is strong evidence that the worker is an employee. Periodic or on-going training about procedures and methods is even stronger evidence of an employer-employee relationship. However, independent contractors ordinarily use their own methods.[12]

Be careful about offering or requiring training of your independent contractors. They should come already trained to be able to do their jobs. One homeschool program required their independent contractor teachers to attend an Information Night with the parents. They went over the policies and rules of the co-op. If possible, try to avoid mandatory meetings like these that require your contractors to attend. Give them the policy and rules but avoid "training" them. Of course it would be wonderful if the contract teacher came to the Information Night to meet the parents and students, but do not make attendance mandatory. Invite your contract teachers, but do not require attendance.

One co-op leader had parents willing to teach, but several felt under-prepared to manage a classroom. The co-op coordinated with other homeschool programs in the area and conducted a Tutor Training Workshop. It was completely optional for the independent contractors to attend. The independent contractors who did attend paid for the workshop, much like I pay for my continuing education classes as a CPA. This may be training, but because it was optional, the tutors remained as independent contractors.

FINANCIAL CONTROL

The IRS explains the second factor in determining worker classification is Financial Control which covers whether the business has a right to direct or control the financial aspects of the worker's job. This includes:

Unreimbursed Expenses

The extent to which the worker has unreimbursed business expenses. Independent contractors are more likely to have unreimbursed expenses than are employees. Fixed ongoing costs that are incurred regardless of whether work is currently being performed are especially important. However, employees may also incur unreimbursed expenses in connection with the services that they perform for their business.

In your independent contractor agreement be clear about what expenses your homeschool program will reimburse. For example, one homeschool group hired a fantastic music teacher. She requested mileage reimbursement because she had to travel over 30 miles to teach at the co-op. The co-op included that in her independent contractor agreement. Employees are not reimbursed for commuting miles.

Investment in Equipment

An independent contractor often has a significant investment in the equipment he or she uses in working for someone else. There are no precise dollar limits that must be met in order to have a significant investment. Furthermore, a significant investment is not necessary for independent contractor status as some types of work simply do not require large expenditures.

Frequently teachers in a homeschool program do not have a lot invested in equipment. They show up and teach. Some may have books or supplies, but there is no need for an independent contractor to make a significant expenditure to be hired to teach.

Services Available to the Market

The extent to which the worker makes his or her services available to the relevant market. An independent contractor is generally free to seek out business opportunities. Independent contractors often advertise, maintain a visible business location, and are available to work in the relevant market.

This factor seems to be a key factor in worker determination. One co-op hired two people: one for teaching band and one as co-op director. The band director was employed in the marketplace (a private school) as a band teacher and taught music lessons to several children, making his status as an independent contractor pretty clear. On the other hand, a co-op director is not usually working for other co-ops and should probably be hired as an employee.

How Worker is Paid

An employee is generally guaranteed a regular wage amount for an hourly, weekly, or other period of time. This usually indicates that a worker is an employee, even when the wage or salary is supplemented by a commission. An independent contractor is usually paid by a flat fee for the job. However, it is common in some professions, such as law, to pay independent contractors hourly.

Sometimes I charge clients by the hour for my CPA consultations. That does not mean I am their employee. But I encourage homeschool groups to pay their independent contractors by the job, not by the hour. I recommend that homeschool groups negotiate a semester rate, not an hourly rate, with contract teachers.

Worker Can Make a Profit or a Loss

The extent to which the worker can realize a profit or incur a loss. The opportunity to make a profit or loss is another important factor. If a worker has a significant investment in the tools and equipment used and if the worker has unreimbursed expenses, the worker has a greater opportunity to lose money (i.e., their expenses will exceed their income from the work). Having the possibility of incurring a loss indicates that the worker is an independent contractor.[13]

It's pretty rare for a homeschool teacher to actually lose money by teaching, but, as much as possible, I encourage homeschool groups to shift the financial risk to the independent contractor. One way to do this is to negotiate payment based on class size. The smaller the class, the lower the payment to the contract teacher. That way if only two students sign up the independent contractor will receive lower pay and may even incur a loss.

One co-op wanted to please their contractor teachers and agreed to pay them a minimum price even if class enrollment was low. While generous, I discourage this practice because the independent contractor is supposed to bear the financial risk, not your homeschool program. Additionally, avoiding a guaranteed minimum pay will incentivize the teacher of provide a quality course to attract more students. Of course, if the pay is too low the teacher may quit so you may need to have an open and honest negotiation. But always keep in mind that the independent contractor should run the risk of financial loss, not your organization.

Type of Relationship

The IRS describes the third factor it uses in making a worker classification: the type of relationship.

Type of relationship[14] refers to facts that show how the worker and business perceive their relationship to each other. The factors for the type of relationship between two parties generally fall into the categories of:

- Written contracts
- Employee benefits
- Permanency of the relationship
- Services provided as key activity of the business

Written Contracts

Although a contract may state that the worker is an employee or an independent contractor, this is not sufficient to determine the worker's status. The IRS is not required to follow a contract stating that the worker is an independent contractor, responsible for paying his or her own self-employment tax. How the parties work together determines whether the worker is an employee or an independent contractor.

I strongly encourage having an independent contractor agreement and include several samples in Chapter 8: Sample Independent Contractor Agreements. The IRS even states, that "A written contract specifying employee or independent contractor status is important evidence."[15] But the IRS is quite clear that your actions and behavior to your independent contractor speak louder than any paper you sign.

Employee Benefits

Employee benefits include things like insurance, pension plans, paid vacation, sick days, and disability insurance. Businesses generally do not grant these benefits to independent contractors. However, the lack of these types of benefits does not necessarily mean the worker is an independent contractor

I cover benefits, especially free or reduced tuition for the independent contractors, in Chapter 4: Guidelines for Hiring Independent Contractors.

Permanency of the Relationship

If you hire a worker with the expectation that the relationship will continue indefinitely, rather than for a specific project or period, this is generally considered evidence that the intent was to create an employer-employee relationship.

Always have start and end dates in your independent contractor agreements.

Services Provided as Key Activity of the Business

If a worker provides services that are a key aspect of the business, it is more likely that the business will have the right to direct and control his or her activities. For example, if a law firm hires an attorney, it is likely that it will present the attorney's work as its own and would have the right to control or direct that work. This would indicate an employer-employee relationship.[16]

This final factor, services provided as key activity of the business, is a very important factor for many homeschool organizations. Frequently, the teachers, tutors, or coaches hired to teach in a homeschool program are a key aspect of the homeschool program. Without these teachers, many homeschool programs would not exist. If a homeschool organization's academic program is conducted largely by paid teachers, then there is a strong indication that they are employees, not independent contractors.

But if, instead, a homeschool organization's classes are largely taught by volunteer parents and only a handful of teachers are paid, then the paid teachers are not a key aspect of the program and are more likely to be independent contractors. Additionally, homeschool program directors should be classified as employees because they provide key services to the organization.

Remember to Weigh All the Factors:

The IRS reminds employers that:

> Businesses must weigh all these factors when determining whether a worker is an employee or independent contractor. Some factors may indicate that the worker is an employee, while other factors indicate that the worker is an independent contractor. **There is no "magic" or set number of factors that "makes" the worker an employee or an independent contractor, and no one factor stands alone in making this determination.** Also, factors which are relevant in one situation may not be relevant in another. (Emphasis added.)

> The keys are to look at the entire relationship, consider the degree or extent of the right to direct and control, and finally, to document each of the factors used in coming up with the determination. [17]

To summarize the IRS guidelines in making worker classification, it's complicated. No one factor weighs more heavily than another. There is no magic number or overriding factor. Each case is different and unique and each must be decided on a case-by-case basis.

That being said, I will introduce you to the former method the IRS used to make a worker classification. It may help bring clarity to your situation.

A Test to Determine Worker Status

In the past, the IRS used a 20 factor test to determine employee or independent contractor status (see www.irs.gov/taxtopics/tc762.html

). This test has been replaced by three broader criteria discussed earlier, but the 20 factor test is still useful for determining worker status.

Although this is a useful tool, be aware that the IRS does not use a set guideline such as 12 out of 20 "yes" answers is an employee and the factors are not weighted equally. Use this test to guide you in making your worker classification.

1. **Instructions.** Workers who must comply with your instructions as to when, where, and how they work are more likely to be employees. Naturally, when you hire a teacher for your homeschool program, you will tell her when and where the class meets, but the emphasis here is on giving instructions on how to do her job.

2. **Training.** The more training you give or require of workers, the more likely it is that they are employees. Independent contractors know how to do their work and should not require training in how to deliver their services. A homeschool co-op wanted their tutors trained in classical methods of instruction. They can ask potential tutors if they understand the classical education model, but should not provide or require mandatory training. One homeschool program offered training, but it was strictly voluntary and they charged a fee to all attendees, parents and contract teacher alike.

3. **Integration.** The more important that your workers' services are to your organization's success or continuation, the more likely it is that they're employees. If a homeschool organization depends heavily on their tutors to conduct classes, then those tutors are more likely to be employees. But if a homeschool co-op is staffed primarily with parent-volunteers doing the teaching and only a few hired teachers, then the hired teachers are more likely to be independent contractors.

4. **Services rendered personally.** If you require your hired worker to personally perform the services, then it is more

likely that he or she is an employee. But, instead, if you allow your teacher to send a substitute, she is more likely to be an independent contractor. A homeschool program in Texas allowed substitutes in their teacher agreement. They asked the teacher to provide a substitute (with prior approval by the co-op) if she was sick or would be absent. That teacher was more likely to be an independent contractor.

5. **Hiring assistants.** An independent contractor may hire his or her own assistants. An employee does not hire or pay their own assistants. A coach working for a homeschool program hired a student assistant to help him teach sports classes. The coach paid the assistant himself. This made the coach more likely to be an independent contractor.

6. **Continuing relationship.** If your workers have been with your organization for a long period of time and return year after year, it is more likely that they are employees. Your contractor agreement, words, and actions should be very clear that there is no guarantee of a continued relationship for independent contractors.

7. **Set hours of work.** Employees usually work set hours. Independent contractors usually can set their own work hours. But having preset hours is very typical for homeschool co-op teachers. They are hired to teach a class that meets at a specific time each week. Having scheduled teaching times does not automatically make the teacher an employee.

8. **Full time required.** If you require a worker to work or be available full time, it is likely he or she is an employee. In contrast, independent contractors generally can work whenever and for whomever they choose.

9. **Work done on premises.** Independent contractors usually have their own place of business where they can do their work for you. Employees usually work at your premises or at a place

you designate. Teachers in a homeschool co-op would be expected to teach where the co-op meets, but they could still be classified as independent contractors.

10. **Order or sequence set.** Workers for whom you set the order or sequence in which they perform their services are more likely employees.

11. **Reports.** Workers whom you require to submit oral or written reports are more likely employees.

12. **Payment method.** Workers paid by the hour, week, or month are more likely employees. Independent contractors are usually paid by the job.

13. **Expenses.** If you pay business and travel expenses for a worker, it is more likely that he or she is an employee. Independent contractors are usually expected to cover their own expenses.

14. **Tools and materials.** Independent contractors provide their own tools and supplies. Employees use tools, materials, and other equipment that you furnish. Does your homeschool co-op have a supply closet with craft, paper, and office supplies? Be sure that these supplies are only used by the co-op members and not the independent contractors.

15. **Investment.** Independent contractors usually have made some investment in their business. As an independent contractor, I pay for my professional business license and required continuing education each year. Another CPA who works as an employee of an accounting firm has her licensing expenses paid by the firm. She makes no investment of her own as an employee.

16. **Profit or loss.** An independent contractor should have some risk in making a profit or loss in rendering their services. Teaching, coaching, or providing bookkeeping services to a

homeschool organization will rarely result in a loss, but these workers may still be considered independent contractors.

17. **Works for more than one person at a time.** The more businesses for which your workers perform services at the same time, the more likely it is that they're independent contractors. Homeschool co-op teachers may work for more than one person. They may tutor several students in addition to teaching at your co-op. In contrast, homeschool co-op directors rarely work for more than one co-op at a time and it is more likely that they are employees.

18. **Services available to general public.** Workers who offer their services out to the general public are more likely independent contractors.

19. **Right to fire.** Workers whom you can fire at any time are more likely employees. In contrast, your right to terminate an independent contractor is limited to the terms of your agreement (that's why you need a good independent contractor agreement).

20. **Right to quit.** Workers who can quit at any time without incurring any liability to you are more likely employees. In contrast, independent contractors generally cannot quit in the middle of a job. If a contractor quits in the middle of the semester, she runs the risk of being held financially accountable for her failure to complete the job. Your independent contractor agreement may have some financial penalty for quitting early such as forfeiting a month of compensation.

20 Factor Checklist

You may prefer this checklist of the 20 factors the IRS used to determine worker classification. A Yes answer is more likely that a worker is an employee. A No answer is more likely that the worker is an independent contractor. And, of course, some factors may not apply to your situation.

	Yes/ EE	No/ IC	N/A
Worker must comply with instructions.			
Worker is trained by organization.			
Worker's services are integrated in business.			
Worker must personally render services.			
Worker cannot hire or fire assistants.			
Work relationship is continuous or indefinite.			
Work hours are preset. (See Note 1)			
Worker must devote full time to this business.			
Work is done on the employer's premises. (See Note 2)			
Worker cannot control order or sequence of work.			
Worker submits oral or written reports.			
Worker is paid at specific intervals (hourly, weekly, etc.).			
Worker's business expenses are reimbursed.			
Worker is provided with tools or materials.			
Worker has no significant investment in the business.			
Worker has no opportunity for profit/loss.			
Worker is not engaged by many different firms. (See Note 3)			
Worker does not offer services to public. (See Note 3)			

Worker may be discharged or fired by employer.			
Worker can terminate without liability.			

Note 1: Having preset hours is very typical for homeschool co-op teachers. They are hired to teach a class that meets at a specific time each week. Having scheduled teaching times does not automatically make the teacher an employee.

Note 2: It is quite common for contractors to work at the employer's premises, so this factor does not automatically make the worker an employee.

Note 3: Offering services to the public weighs quite heavily in the IRS worker classification decision. A person who works solely for your homeschool organization might be deemed an employee.

OTHER GOVERNMENT AGENCIES ALSO DETERMINE WORKER STATUS

A homeschool leader from Texas contacted me in a panic. She had called the Texas Workforce Commission (TWC) to get clarity on the independent contractors who taught classes in her homeschool co-op. The state employee was quite emphatic that her teachers were employees. She emailed me asking,

> "As we look over the IRS 20 factor test to determine employee vs. independent contractor, we can sway either way depending on the interpretation of the points. Does it all boil down to the TWC and their perspective? Who does the buck stop with and who has the final say?

In truth, there are several governmental agencies at the federal and state level that each get their say in how a worker is classified. **No one has final say; all the various government agencies can each have different factors in making a worker classification.**

US DEPARTMENT OF LABOR

The United States Department of Labor (DOL) also makes worker determination. Their focus is on minimum wage and overtime rules. The IRS and DOL have an agreement to coordinate with each other on worker misclassification of employees. That means if the IRS conducts a worker classification audit of your organization, they will alert the DOL to your situation as well.

The governing act the DOL follows is the Fair Labor Standards Act (FLSA). They make determinations of who is an employee and therefore protected under FLSA. The Department of Labor makes a worker determination based on an economic realities test. This test claims that if the worker *depends* on income from the employer, that worker is an employee. That's a very different criteria than what the IRS uses.

The DOL publishes a fact sheet titled, "Am I an Employee?: Employment Relationship Under the Fair Labor Standards Act (FLSA)." It is available at www.dol.gov/whd/regs/compliance/whdfs13.pdf

The fact sheet mentions six factors the DOL uses to determine if a worker is an employee and therefore subject to the FLSA. Some of the factors are very similar to the IRS's three factors. An employee must be paid at least the Federal minimum wage of $7.25 per hour, and overtime at time-and-a-half his or her regular rate of pay for all hours worked in excess of 40 per week.

STATE AGENCIES MAKE WORKER DETERMINATIONS TOO

The United States has a complex government structure. Several federal agencies (such as the IRS and the Department of Labor) have a say in worker determination and each of the 50 states have their own standards for worker classification as well. Additionally, 30 states have agreements with the IRS and DOL to share information related to worker classification. Tax auditors on each side share information with each other, but the states are not bound by the IRS definition of independent contractor. For example, Maryland presumes all workers are employees. A worker is an independent contractor only if the service they provide is "outside the usual course of business."[18] This means that teachers in a homeschool program should be classified as employees because teaching is the normal course of business.

The states care about worker classification because they are largely responsible for operating and funding unemployment compensation and worker's compensation.

A homeschool program in Ohio was audited by the IRS for classifying their teachers as independent contractors. The IRS determined the teachers should be employees. After this group was finished with the IRS audit (it was all conducted by letter, not face-to-face), a call came from the Ohio Office of Unemployment Insurance. They wanted to conduct their own audit and this one was face-to-face! The IRS shares with the states the names of organizations that they audit.

So be aware that your state government will conduct audits of worker classification. This homeschool group did not owe any money to the IRS (see the section on safe harbor rules), but they owed the State of Ohio $3,000 for prior years' unemployment insurance!

CAN'T DECIDE? THE IRS OFFERS TO HELP

The IRS can make a worker classification for your organization if you desire. File IRS Form SS-8 Determination of Worker Status for Purposes of Federal Employment Taxes and Income Tax Withholding (available at the IRS website (www.irs.gov/pub/irs-pdf/fss8.pdf). You will need to provide detailed information about your relationship with the worker including a copy of any agreement you have with the worker, a description of the services the contractor provided, and a description of how you supervise or direct the worker's services and pay for the services.

I recommend that you have the Form SS-8 reviewed by an experienced tax professional or an employment attorney. The worker classification decision is very subjective and you want to be sure that each factor is presented properly and that no material facts are omitted or misleading. An experienced professional can help ensure that each statement in the request reflects your case in its best light.

The Form SS-8 is usually filed by disgruntled workers who thought they should be classified as employees. These workers request the IRS to investigate in hopes of getting employee benefits such as insurance or to avoid paying self-employment tax.

I suggest you consider this option carefully, since you will have to live with the IRS's decision. If they determine you have employees, you will have to file the proper paperwork, follow federal and state laws regarding employees, and pay employment taxes (Social Security, Medicare, unemployment insurance premiums). Your organization may be liable for back taxes from prior years as well. Additionally, your organization may also be liable to your state for unemployment insurance premiums and workers compensation taxes for the years that the workers were misclassified.

IRS OFFERS A SAFE HARBOR FOR WORKER CLASSIFICATION

If the IRS determines your organization has misclassified its workers as independent contractors, there can be tax liabilities for prior years. Fortunately, the IRS does offer a safe harbor, meaning if you follow these rules, your organization will not owe back taxes even if you misclassified your workers.

Section 530 of the Revenue Act of 1978[19] established safe-harbor rules that allow an employer to avoid employment tax liabilities if:

1. Your organization consistently treated the worker and other workers performing similar tasks as independent contractors;

2. Your organization had a reasonable basis for treating the worker as an independent contractor; <u>and</u>

3. Your organization filed all required information returns, such as Form 1099-MISC.

All three provisions must be met to benefit from the safe harbor rules.

That second condition, "reasonable basis" for classifying your work as an independent contractor, has more details. The IRS says that a reasonable basis includes any of the following:

- judicial precedent, published rulings, technical advice or a letter ruling you received from the IRS
- a past audit by the IRS
- long-standing recognized practice of a significant segment of the industry in which the individual works (for example, most workers in your industry are treated as independent contractors by employers)

That last provision will be helpful if your organization is ever audited by the IRS for worker classification. You could probably prove that hiring teachers and tutors as independent contractors is a long-standing practice in the homeschool industry.

In other words, if you have always treated a worker as an independent contractor and properly filed the corresponding tax returns (Form 1099-MISC), you can take advantage of the safe harbor rules and avoid prior year tax liabilities.

This happened to a homeschool organization in Ohio I mentioned earlier. The IRS determined that the workers (all part-time teachers in a homeschool tutorial program) were employees, not independent contractors. The homeschool organization reclassified their teachers as employees. The homeschool program had met all the criteria of the safe harbor rules including giving all their teachers 1099-MISC forms every year, so they did not owe any prior year employment taxes or penalties. Although they did not like the IRS audit determination, at least they didn't owe any taxes or penalties. Lesson learned: give your independent contractors a 1099-MISC every year and keep copies for yourself!

FAQ on Worker Classification

Q: We are forming a nonprofit homeschool band. We will charge a monthly tuition which will cover compensating the band director for directing the band. The band director teaches at another business. He is planning on forming an LLC. He gets a percentage of each student's monthly tuition (he quoted us the percentage he wanted). Would he be considered an employee or an independent contractor?

A: There is not enough information for me to make a proper determination, but you did tell me three things that seem to imply that your band director could be classified as an independent contractor:

1. He teaches at another business.
2. He is setting himself up as a business owner "planning on forming an LLC."
3. He is not paid by the hour. "He gets a percentage of each student's monthly tuition."

But there are many other factors to consider, mainly how much control your organization will have over him and his work. If you determine he is an independent contractor, then I strongly advise you to have a written contract with him and clearly spell out that he is hired as an independent contractor and responsible for his own taxes. Have him fill out a W-9 so that you have his legal name and Social Security Number or Employer Identification Number.

Q: If we have a written and signed agreement with our independent contractor, won't we be safe?

A: Employers are mistaken when they believe that they are "safe" simply by having their workers sign agreements that declare the workers to be independent contractors. Such agreements carry little, if any, weight with the IRS, Department of Labor, or state governments. If your actions show an employee relationship, then your workers are employees regardless of what you call them or any signed agreement. In other words, actions speak louder than written words.

Q: The worker we hired wants to be treated as an independent contractor. Is that good enough basis to treat him like an independent contractor?

A: No. You should not assume it is safe to classify a worker as an independent contractor simply because the worker wanted, or asked, to be treated as an independent contractor. Your relationship and behavior count more than the worker's desires.

Q: Are Classical Conversations (CC) tutors employees or independent contractors? As a CC Director I have all my tutors sign an agreement to be independent contractors.

A: It is not easy to answer this question. Having a contract is not assurance that a tutor is an independent contractor; how they are treated and the amount of control you exert over them is the determining factor. From what I have seen and know of CC tutors, their services are a key activity of the business. That alone could cause the IRS to determine that CC tutors are employees.

Q: I own and operate a homeschool tutorial program. It is not a non-profit. Do I give myself a paycheck?

A: It depends on the business structure your chose for your business. Most businesses are sole proprietorships and a sole proprietor does not give herself a paycheck. All the profits belong to the owner and she reports them on her individual tax return Form 1040 Schedule

C Business Income or Loss. You may withdraw money from the business checking account and transfer it to your personal bank account. This is called an "owner's draw," but it is not a paycheck. It is merely drawing the profits out of the business for your personal use. You, as owner, do not give yourself a W-2. The taxes you owe are all reported on the Form 1040. Be sure to set aside some money to pay your taxes; don't withdraw every penny.

If your business was formed as an S Corporation, then you will issue yourself a paycheck for the hours you worked in the business. This can be confusing and complicated. Please consult a local CPA or schedule a consultation with me at HomeschoolCPA.com/Contact.

Q: You seem to know a lot about worker classification, Carol. Will you help us determine if our workers are independent contractors or employees?

A: I can assist homeschool organizations in making a worker classification determinations. I offer a telephone consultation and follow up with a determination and recommendations of changes your group should make if needed. Visit HomeschoolCPA.com/Services to arrange a consultation to discuss your worker classification determination.

Q: Should I hire an attorney?

A: You could certainly hire an attorney, especially if you request the IRS to make a worker classification determination for you by submitting Form SS-8 Determination of Worker Status. The IRS determination is very subjective, so you want an experienced professional to advise you.

[4]

Chapter 4: Guidelines for Hiring Independent Contractors

I hope Chapter 3 has helped you determine if your organization's worker is an employee or an independent contractor. Now you are ready for some guidelines, rules, and laws affecting each type of worker. In this chapter I will offer guidelines for independent contractors and in Chapter 6: Payroll Taxes for Employers I will explain the rules for employees.

TAXES

Remind your contractor that your homeschool organization will not be withholding income taxes, Social Security or Medicare taxes. Independent contractors are business owners and they are responsible for paying federal income tax and both halves of Social Security and Medicare taxes (it's called self-employment tax and paid along with their federal income tax on IRS Form 1040). This may come as quite a shock to the independent contractor when she prepares her tax return, especially if she has earned a large amount. Warn your independent contractors in writing, verbally, and in the independent contractor agreement that no taxes will be withheld.

Equipment and Supplies

Independent contractors generally bring and use their own equipment and supplies. This should be mentioned in the independent contractor agreement. Clearly state what expenses your organization will reimburse, but it should be minimal and with restrictions. Perhaps your homeschool co-op will reimburse for art supplies or a teacher's manual that the co-op keeps as their own. Your co-op should request that prior approval be granted before the independent contractor makes a purchase for which she wants to be reimbursed. You don't want to be surprised with a request for reimbursement that you never approved! If an independent contractor buys supplies and requests reimbursement, your organization should check if it is mentioned in the agreement before making a payment.

For example, Heather was hired to teach an art class as an independent contractor for a homeschool organization. The agreement stated this:

> The Independent Contractor will provide all necessary supplies and equipment. The Independent Contractor will provide parents a list of art supplies each student needs. Parents will make these purchases. Reimbursable purchases are limited to supplies that the entire class will use. Prior approval from the Co-op Director is required before making a reimbursable purchase.

Heather used her own art supplies and equipment to make samples of each art project. She also had to buy a few additional art supplies to make the samples. Heather is free to keep these supplies as her own property. She can claim them as a business deduction on her income tax return. Additionally, Heather bought one supply for the entire class to use (a spray can of paint). She asked the director for approval of this purchase before she bought it. Then Heather requested reimbursement for the paint and gave it to the co-op after the class ended. If Heather wanted to keep the paint for herself, she would not be reimbursed.

ASSISTANTS

Independent contractors can hire their own assistants, but frequently a homeschool program prefers to supply a classroom assistant, usually a volunteer parent. This keeps costs down and also gives the homeschool program control over who is involved in teaching the students. If your homeschool group will provide a classroom assistant, be sure the independent contractor knows that. Include a statement in the agreement, such as:

> A volunteer classroom assistant will be provided. If the Independent Contractor wishes to hire an assistant, he or she must be approved by the Co-op Director and provide a background check to the Co-op Director.

SUBSTITUTES

Sometimes an independent contractor is ill and needs to have a substitute teacher. Work out the details about what to do if the independent contractor needs a substitute. Who provides the substitute, the independent contractor or your homeschool organization? Will the substitute be the volunteer classroom assistant? Does your homeschool group want to approve the substitute teacher beforehand? Will the substitute be paid by the independent contractor or by your organization? Mention these issues in the independent contractor agreement.

EVALUATIONS

Do not evaluate an independent contractor teacher on his or her teaching methods. An independent contractor is evaluated on results—the end product—not the procedures used. This does not mean you should not keep an eye on how the teacher is performing. Obviously, your organization may need to step in if classroom management is a concern since it will affect the outcome. A chaotic, poorly managed class means the students cannot learn and the independent contractor is not performing her agreed-to services.

Do not perform an evaluation similar to an employee feedback session. Employees can be evaluated on their methods, but not independent contractors; they are evaluated only on their results. For example, an employee could be evaluated on friendliness, student engagement, flexibility, communication, planning, etc. An independent contractor can only be evaluated on the result: did she show up to teach the class? If you find yourself with a checklist of performance criteria for your teachers, you may be treating that teacher as an employee.

TRAINING

Training for independent contractors should be minimal or none at all. Independent contractors should already possess all the education and skills required to perform their services and not need additional training. If you need to train a worker, he may need to be classified as an employee.

I was hired as an independent contractor to teach a class in personal finance at a homeschool organization. I was surprised when I received an email late in the summer about full-day required training. This training was on the goals and visions of the organization and in how to teach using classical methods. I told the director that as an independent contractor, I was sufficiently trained in the content of the class (personal finance), I could read about the vision of the organization, but that required training in the *methods* of teaching was out of line to request from an independent contractor. I thought that the organization was treating independent contractors as employees. Nothing changed that year (I attended the training anyway), but a few years later the organization reclassified all their independent contractors as employees and continued the required training in the methods of teaching.

PAYMENT

Contractors are paid by the job, not (usually) by the hour. Your homeschool organization should avoid paying an independent contractor on an hourly basis. The total fee may be based on the number of hours spent teaching, but the independent contractor agreement should state the entire fee, not an hourly fee.

For example, a homeschool program hired a Spanish teacher. The treasurer determined that $20 per class session was a reasonable fee to pay the Spanish teacher. The treasurer calculated that 10 class sessions at $20 each would be a $200 payment to the teacher for the semester, and that was offered to her. The Spanish teacher requested $250. The homeschool program board agreed, and the total fee of $250 for 10 classes was put in the agreement. No mention of an hourly rate was put in the independent contractor agreement.

FINANCIAL RISK

A contractor should have some financial risk. Often providing services such as teaching or bookkeeping does not involve much risk of financial loss, but as much as possible, shift some risk to your independent contractors. For example, a homeschool co-op offered to pay a teacher a set amount of money to teach a class regardless of the number of students who signed up to take the class. Instead the independent contractor should have had the risk of not earning much if student enrollment was low or earning more if enrollment was high. Having an agreement that the independent contractor is paid on a per-student basis shifts some of the risk onto the teacher. I'm not advising that all homeschool co-ops shift to a per-student compensation model for independent contractors, but it is a way to shift some financial risk to the independent contractor.

Work Elsewhere

Contractors frequently advertise and are considered free to take work from other companies. Employees usually have to work for a single employer only.

A homeschool organization planned to hire two workers, a childcare worker and a co-op administrator who would be in charge of the daily operation of the homeschool classes. The childcare worker was a freelance babysitter, working for several families. In contrast, the co-op administrator did not provide her services to anyone else. She is more likely to be classified as an employee based on this and several other factors.

No Benefits

Avoid offering your independent contractors any benefits including reduced fees, discounted tuition, or free nursery care for their baby. Independent contractors should not be given paid sick days, paid vacation days or other paid time off.

Defined Time

Set a time frame for the agreement. Renew it every year or every semester. Do not leave the contract open-ended.

INTELLECTUAL PROPERTY

If the independent contractor is creating art, curriculum, a written work, photographs, or other creative works, then *they* own the copyright to works created as a contractor, not your homeschool group. If your homeschool organization wants the rights to the created work (especially curriculum), create a separate contract outlining ownership of the work. The agreement should be clear that the independent contractor is working-for-hire, and he or she forfeits the copyright. For more information on copyrights and work for hire visit www.writersandeditors.com and click on "Copyright, work for hire, and other rights issues."

AVOID CONTROLLING YOUR INDEPENDENT CONTRACTOR

If your group would like to exert some control over teachers such as choosing curriculum or class content, requiring teachers to attend training sessions, or evaluating their performance, then you should pay them as employees.

One homeschool co-op was very particular about what method of teaching and content was taught to their students. They picked the curriculum and required training in their methods and their view of instruction. Then they evaluated the teachers on their teaching style, control of the classroom, and engagement with the students. They may be too controlling for their teachers to be accurately classified as independent contractors. They could increase the likelihood of properly treating the teachers as independent contractors by hiring teachers who are already trained in their methods and views of instruction, not require training (i.e., make it optional), and change their evaluation to focus on the completion of the tasks listed in their agreement and not focus on the teacher's style of teaching. Or they could hire the teacher as an employee.

How Much Control is Too Much? The Plumber Test

How much you can control an independent contractor is a very difficult question to answer, because every situation is unique. Consider the model of a plumber when thinking about control and independent contractors. A plumber is an independent contractor who is hired for a specific, temporary job: to fix your plumbing. You usually have an informal, verbal agreement and may get an estimate of the cost before he begins work. He comes to your house at an agreed-upon time and brings his own tools. You may show him the problem and be in the room while he works, but you do not tell him how to do his job. You assume he knows what tools to use. He may return for additional work and will invoice you.

Now compare the plumber model to your relationship with your homeschool program's independent contractors. Does it look like the plumber model? Then you are treating your independent contractors properly. If instead you exert more control over your workers than you do a plumber, then consider reclassifying them as employees.

Have a Written Agreement with Your Independent Contractor

A signed contractor agreement is important and highly recommended (see Chapter 8 for samples). It serves to clarify to the worker her status as an independent contractor. But a signed agreement will *not* secure independent contractor status. All the factors mentioned earlier are still important in determining worker status. In a letter to a homeschool nonprofit that used contractor agreements, the IRS wrote:

> For federal employment tax purposes, it is the actual working relationship that is controlling and not the terms of the contract between the parties.

Use signed agreements, but remember your behavior and relationship to that worker carries more weight in worker determination than a signed agreement. In other words, actions speak louder than words.

When preparing an agreement between your homeschool organization and an independent contractor (I'm using a teacher in the bullet points below), include the following:

- A clearly written agreement signed by both parties.
- A request for necessary tax information by requiring a Form W-9 be given to the homeschool organization before the teacher will be paid.
- A well-defined scope of work. Be specific and list the title of the class the teacher will teach.
- A clear statement that the hired worker is an independent contractor and ineligible for benefits.
- A statement that the teacher decides how the work is to be performed.
- A requirement that the teacher will submit an invoice to the homeschool organization for payment.
- A statement of the total fee for the job. If several payments are made (i.e., monthly), state the frequency. Avoid hourly payments if possible. Compensation should not look like a salary; it is a total payment for services.
- The worker will provide her own tools, books, and equipment.
- Define if the teacher has freedom to contract with others to perform the services. Describe who will be a substitute for her. Usually an independent contractor may assign others to perform the duties outlined in the scope of the agreement, but most homeschool groups reserve the right to approve of the substitute or provide a substitute from their participants.

- Termination rights for nonperformance or breach of contract. Some faith-based homeschool groups also reserve the right to terminate for failure to follow a code of conduct or for making statements in violation of the statement of faith. But requiring an independent contractor to agree to your statement of faith or code of conduct could mean you are overly controlling and should hire them as an employee.

This list above (with some of my comments added) was taken from a very helpful PowerPoint presentation "Focus on Nonprofit Employee Misclassification" made by Venable LLP. You may want to read through the slides yourself. The link is in the Endnotes.[20]

HOW YOU PAY YOUR IC MAY AFFECT THE PROPERTY TAX EXEMPTION FOR YOUR HOST CHURCH

Several homeschool leaders have recently learned that the way their homeschool groups are compensating the teachers (parents paying teachers directly) may jeopardize the property tax exemption of their host churches.

THE PROBLEM

Some state laws limit churches renting their building for business purposes to only a few days a year. One homeschool program arranged for teachers to conduct classes for homeschooled children each week for about 30 weeks of the year. They held the classes in a church. Each teacher was paid by the parents, so each teacher was essentially a business owner, not an employee of the homeschool program. The church was hosting a business every time the homeschool program met and therefore was exceeded the state-set limit on business activities.

This situation can put a church's property tax exemption in jeopardy. The church is more likely to stop hosting the homeschool group than to give up property tax exemption. If churches across the United States stopped hosting homeschool programs, it could mean the end of many homeschool programs and render a blow to homeschooling across the country.

What Can a Homeschool Group Do?

I recommend that homeschool organizations in this situation begin collecting the money from the parents and pay the teachers as employees or independent contractors hired by the homeschool group. Many homeschool organizations are 501(c)(3) educational nonprofits. State laws usually allow a church to rent space to a nonprofit if they have a charitable, educational, or religious purpose and not be considered as hosting a business.

It's more work for the board to manage the payments to the teachers and for the treasurer to prepare the checks and IRS forms, but it keeps the homeschool program running and protects the church's property tax exemption.

Can This Happen to My Homeschool Group?

Here are some issues for all homeschool organizations who conduct classes in churches to consider:

- Be aware of the limits on business activities conducted by churches in your state's property tax exemption laws. There may be no limits or a set number of days that a church can host a business.
- Talk to your host church about this issue. Ask what they know about limits on business activity for churches.
- If your state's property tax laws limit your host church, consider changing how your teachers are paid so that the church is not renting space for business activities to for-profit businesses (i.e., individual teachers).

- Be sure your activities are in line with the religious and charitable purposes of your host church.

Note that this affects a church's **property** tax exemption, not their income tax exemption at the federal or state levels.

FAQ ON INDEPENDENT CONTRACTORS

Q: We are a homeschool co-operative program and all our teachers are volunteers. I collect on their behalf fee to help cover costs related to teaching: curriculum, printing handouts and lesson plans, etc. This amount is determined by the teacher, usually $10 to $50 per semester. These funds are collected and then given to the instructor at the beginning of the semester. We don't require receipts or an accounting to be submitted. Any remaining funds are considered a "donation" to the teacher to recognize their time and effort in teaching the class. Teachers are not required to refund monies back to the families. Most of us feel that this structure is reasonable. However, one member is questioning.

A: When you do not request receipts, you are running what the IRS calls a "non-accountable" plan for reimbursements. Under a non-accountable plan, the full amount given to the teachers is taxable income. The remaining funds that you let your teachers keep are not a donation; it is a payment for services and is taxable income that needs to be reported to the IRS. Your homeschool co-op should be giving the teachers a W-2 or a 1099-MISC. Or you should change your practices to follow an accountable plan by requiring receipts and the return of unspent monies. Read my book *Money Management in a Homeschool Organization* for more information on accountable plans.

Q: I'm a paid teacher offering art classes at a homeschool co-op. I have a signed agreement that I would earn $500 for the semester for

teaching the class. At the end of the year three parents gave me thank you notes with gift cards that totaled $75. Is this taxable income?

A: Probably not. These appear to be genuine gifts of appreciation from parents to you as an individual and not payment for services. Additionally, the gift cards came from parents and not the homeschool co-op that paid you, affirming that they were gifts of appreciation. Gifts this small are not taxable income.

Q: I'm hired as an independent contractor to teach algebra twice a week in a homeschool program. I was told I would be paid $800 for the semester. Some students needed extra attention, and I helped these students outside of class but never asked for payment from the parents or the homeschool group. At the end of the year the program named me teacher of the year and gave me flowers and a gift card worth $50. Is that gift card taxable income?

A: This seems to be a gift from the organization in appreciation for you being an outstanding teacher. But because you are an independent contractor and the money came from the organization, not individuals, the IRS would probably see this $50 as compensation—a bonus—and therefore taxable income. So, just to be safe, I'd follow the IRS guidelines and report any gift cards as taxable compensation.

Q: Some of our paid teachers who have kids in our homeschool program owe our group money. Can we just reduce their salary to reflect their debt to us? For example, one of our teachers will make $1,000 for teaching next semester, but she will owe us $1,588 for all of her kids' classes. Can I just bill her for $588 and call it a day? Another teacher might make $2,000 and owe $1,000. Can we just offer a salary of $1,000?

A: Oh I wish things were as simple as you describe! Unfortunately, for the teachers you pay, you cannot simply net what they owe you with what you owe them. The reason has to do with taxes. Earned income from teaching is taxable income, but tuition the teacher pays to your homeschool program is not a tax deduction. Being paid for rendering services is one transaction (earning taxable income). Paying tuition (which is a personal expense like food or clothing and not tax deductible) is another transaction. The two do not negate each other.

The correct method would be for the homeschool group to pay a contract teacher with a paycheck, and then she pays her tuition fee as a separate transaction.

[5]

Chapter 5: Tax Forms for Independent Contractors

After you establish a worker is properly classified as an independent contractor, there are two documents the Internal Revenue Service (IRS) requires you give to your worker. One, the Form W-9, is given to the independent contractor before he or she begins work for you, and the other, Form 1099-MISC, is given after the end of the calendar year.

Form W-9

Give a Form W-9 Request for Taxpayer Identification Number to each independent contractor to collect his or her legal name and Social Security Number. The information is used by your organization to prepare tax-reporting forms at the end of the year. The W-9 is retained by your organization and not mailed to the IRS.

Form W-9 asks for the independent contractor's name; address; business name (if different); business entity (individual/sole proprietorship, partnership, corporation, limited liability company or "other"); and the contractor's Social Security number (for sole proprietorships that don't use a separate tax ID number) or Employer Identification Number (EIN).

Form W-9 also asks the person filling it out to certify that he or she is exempt from backup withholding. Most taxpayers are exempt, but if they are not (the IRS will notify them), your organization will need to withhold income tax from that contractor's pay at a flat rate of 28% and send it to the IRS.

Since Form W-9 contains an EIN or Social Security number your organization must guard the form carefully to protect against identity theft. Keep it in a secure place; it does not get sent to the IRS.

W-9 Before Being Paid

I recommend that your organization do not pay an independent contractor until a W-9 form is completed and signed. This is a common business practice. This assures that your organization will have the correct legal name and tax identification number from every worker that you will need at tax time.

Additionally, requesting a Form W-9 signals to the worker that your organization follows the tax reporting rules and will not engage in any "under-the-table" or off-the-books payments. In essence, you are telling them that your organization will be reporting all income paid to them to the IRS.

FORM 1099-MISC

The second document your organization will give to an independent contractor is the IRS Form 1099-MISC. This form reports the total compensation the worker receives so that she can correctly prepare her income tax return. The 1099-MISC form is used to report several types of income including rent, royalties, prizes and awards. The most popular use of the form is to report earnings to an independent contractor.

WHO GETS A 1099-MISC

In a homeschool organization the most common type of independent contractor is usually a paid teacher. But other workers may need to be given a 1099-MISC as well. If you hire a cleaning person, someone to set up a website, or a graphic designer, they should be given a 1099-MISC. Professionals, such as an accountant to advise you, may need to be given a 1099-MISC if paid more than $600 in a calendar year. Attorneys and law offices get a 1099-MISC even if they receive less than $600 in compensation for a year. So if you paid an attorney only $200, you still give him a 1099-MISC.

Some examples of independent contractors a homeschool group might compensate include:

Teachers

Hall monitors

Cleaner

Speaker

Entertainer for an event

Web designer

Graphic designer

Bookkeeper

Accountant

Attorney

Board members who are not officers (See Chapter 2: Paying Board Members and Other Leaders)

Corporations do *not* need to be given a 1099-MISC. You can tell if a service provider is a corporation by requesting a Form W-9 and seeing if the box for corporation is checked. For example, I hired a web designer and paid him $700. I requested a W-9 and it came back filled in like this:

John's business is a corporation, so I did not need to issue him a 1099-MISC even though he was paid more than $600 during the year.

COMPENSATION REPORTED ON THE 1099-MISC

At the end of the year, give each contractor who has received total compensation of $600 or more in that year a 1099-MISC form. Recall from Chapters 1 and 2 that compensation includes both payments for services and the value of any taxable benefits, such as free or reduced tuition. Compensation also includes reimbursement of expenses under a nonaccountable plan. A nonaccountable plan is when you do not require an account of the expenses and do not require repayment of unspent monies. Put the total amount of compensation paid during the year in Box 7 Nonemployee compensation.

For example, Brenda was hired as an independent contractor teacher for a homeschool organization and was paid $750 during the year. Additionally, she was given a tuition discount of $150. Her total compensation reported on the Form 1099-MISC in Box 7 Nonemployee compensation is $900 ($750 + $150). Brenda will report the $900 as taxable income on her personal income tax return.

Form 1099-MISC, Miscellaneous Income, 2016. Copy 1 For State Tax Department. Department of the Treasury - Internal Revenue Service.

WHAT IS NOT REPORTED ON 1099-MISC

Reimbursements of expenses are not reported on the 1099-MISC if your organization has an accountable plan for reimbursement. IRS Publication 463 Travel, Entertainment, Gift, and Car Expenses[21] explains an accountable plan must include all of the following rules:

- The expenses must have a business connection — that is, you must have paid or incurred deductible expenses while performing services as an employee or an independent contractor.
- Adequately account for your expenses within 60 days after they were paid or incurred.
- Return any excess reimbursement within 120 days after the expense was paid or incurred.

Mileage expenses can be tricky. It again depends on whether your organization has an accountable plan. Your homeschool organization may reimburse a speaker for her mileage. If the speaker turns in receipts or some record for her mileage, this is considered reimbursement of expenses and not taxable compensation, so no 1099-MISC should be given. For example, I was invited to speak at a homeschool conference. I was offered $500 speaker honorarium and travel reimbursement (mileage). Also provided was a hotel room and a complimentary booth in the vendor hall. I was asked to provide a Google map of the route I took to account for my mileage. I was given two checks, one for the honorarium and another after I accounted for my mileage. My 1099-MISC will show $500, the amount of my taxable compensation. The mileage was reimbursed under an accountable plan (nontaxable) and the hotel and free booth are not taxable compensation.

On the other hand, if your organization does not have an accountable plan, then include the reimbursement of expenses on the Form 1099-MISC.

All this will require good record keeping. See my book *Money Management in a Homeschool Organization* for help with record keeping.

1096 ACCOMPANIES THE FORM 1099-MISC

The Form 1099s are summarized on a cover sheet called the Form 1096. You can see the Form 1096 on the IRS website at www.irs.gov/pub/irs-pdf/f1096.pdf, but you cannot print and file the red ink version. You will need to order official versions or file online.

HOW TO GET 1099/1096 FORMS.

Although you can see the Form 1099-MISC and 1096 online at www.irs.gov/pub/irs-pdf/f1099msc.pdf, you cannot print off the red-ink version of the Form 1099-MISC Copy A (for the IRS) or the Form 1096. The IRS scanners cannot read your home-printed version. You can order copies of the red-ink version from the IRS or buy them at local office supply stores in December. I prefer filing the Forms 1099-MISC online. I use a service called Yearli.com which mails copies to the independent contractors and sends copies to the IRS. See Chapter 9: Resources for a list of online tax form filing services

1099-MISC Due Dates

1099-MISC forms must be given to the independent contractor no later than January 31. Another copy is sent to the IRS either electronically or by paper by January 31 as well. This is a change; employers used to have an additional month to send copies to the IRS. The Form 1099-MISCs are accompanied by a Form 1096. The Form 1096 is a cover page for the 1099-MISC and summarizes the dollar amounts on all the 1099-MISC forms you submit. Retain a copy of the Forms 1099-MISC and 1096 for your records.

Note that the Form 1099-MISC is based on a calendar year, but your organization's operating year or fiscal year may be different. The majority of homeschool organizations operate on a fiscal year that matches the school year, beginning in July or August, but employment tax forms such as the Form 1099-MISC and W-2 are based on a calendar year. So you may hire a teacher for an entire school year, but her payroll tax forms will include portions of two calendar years.

Chapter 6: Payroll Taxes for Employers

Did you know that both nonprofit organizations and for-profit businesses follow the same rules when it comes to employer payroll and taxes? Betty, a homeschool leader in Texas, didn't know this when she emailed me saying,

> "Due to the expenses and paperwork involved with hiring employees, I would like to set up a 501(c)(3)."

I delivered the news Betty probably didn't want to hear: 501(c)(3) tax-exempt status only grants nonprofit organizations tax exemption from federal income tax, not payroll taxes. In other words, **nonprofit tax-exempt organizations still have to pay payroll taxes such as Social Security, Medicare, workers compensation and unemployment insurance premiums**.

To learn more about tax-exempt status for homeschool organizations read *The IRS and Your Homeschool Organization*. See Chapter 9 Resources.

This chapter will explain how to set up a payroll system and the various payroll taxes employers must pay. Chapter 9: Resources lists payroll services, books, videos and websites to help you navigate the tax and legal responsibilities as an employer.

Setting Up a Payroll System

1. **Obtain or find your Employer Identification Number (EIN).** Before hiring employees, you need to get an employment identification number (EIN) from the Internal Revenue Service (IRS). Your organization may already have one. Ask your treasurer or bank. The EIN is necessary for reporting taxes and other documents to the IRS. You can apply for an EIN online at IRS.gov.

2. **Obtain state and local employer IDs.** Some state and local governments require businesses (and nonprofits) to obtain identification numbers in order to process state and local payroll taxes. Intuit (makers of QuickBooks) has compiled a list of state tax agencies on their webpage payroll.intuit.com/state_agencies.

3. **Decide on your pay period.** Setting up a pay period (usually monthly or bi-monthly) is sometimes determined by state law, with most favoring bi-monthly payments (twice a month).

4. **Determine your employee benefits.** Benefits are not typically offered by homeschool organizations who hire part-time and seasonal employees. But you might consider if you will offer paid sick and vacation days (these are not a legal requirement) and if and how you will pay overtime. Overtime pay at one-and-a-half the usual pay rate is only required if employees work more than 40 hours in a week.

5. **Choose a payroll system.** Payroll administration requires acute attention to detail and accuracy, so it's worth doing

some research to understand your options. Typically, your options for managing payroll include doing it yourself or outsourcing to a bookkeeper, accountant or payroll service. However, regardless of the option you choose, you—as the employer—are responsible for reporting and paying all payroll taxes. See Chapter 9: Resources for some payroll services.

6. **Get a W-4 from every employee.** Your employees must fill Form W-4 Federal Income Tax Withholding and return it to you so that you can withhold the correct federal income tax from their pay. See Chapter 7: Tax Forms for Employers for a copy of the Form W-4.

7. **Keep your payroll records.** Federal and some state laws require that employers keep certain records for specified periods of time. For example, W-4 forms must be kept for all active employees and for three years after an employee is terminated. You also need to keep W-2s, copies of filed tax forms, and dates and amounts of all tax deposits.

8. **Report and pay your payroll taxes.** There are several payroll tax reports that you are required to submit to the appropriate authorities on either a quarterly or annual basis. The next section of this book explains payroll taxes. Visit your state tax agency website for state-specific tax filing requirements for employers.

My source for this chapter comes largely from Bizfilings.com, an extremely helpful website run by Wolters Kluwer, a company that provides information on legal, business, tax, and accounting topics. Their Business Owners Toolkit on hiring workers[22] has helpful information. Even if your homeschool organization is a nonprofit and not a business, the BizFilings.com website is helpful, because the payroll tax obligations are the same for nonprofit organizations and for-profit businesses.

EMPLOYER TAXES

If you're a homeschool organization with workers who are employees, your payroll tax obligations will be comprised of the following:

- Federal income tax withholding
- Social Security and Medicare (FICA) taxes
- Federal (FUTA) and state unemployment taxes (SUTA)
- State and sometimes local income taxes

The amount of federal income tax withheld is determined by each employee. The rates for Social Security, Medicare (FICA), and federal unemployment (FUTA) taxes are standard across the United States. The other taxes (SUTA, state and local income tax) vary by state and locality. Additionally, each of these taxes requires payments to be sent at different times, with different forms and to different agencies. See why you want to hire a bookkeeper or payroll service?

FEDERAL INCOME TAX WITHHOLDING

You need to withhold federal income tax from your employee's paycheck if requested by the employee via IRS Form W-4 Employee's Withholding Allowance Certificate. Ideally, the total federal income tax that you withhold from an employee's wages should match what the employee owes in taxes. This matchup is calculated using the Form W-4.

One of the first things you should do whenever you hire a new employee is to have the employee fill out a Form W-4. If you don't have a valid W-4 on file for an employee, you must treat the employee as being single with no exemptions for withholding purposes.

You do not need to mail in the W-4 to the IRS. Instead you keep it for your files. Naturally, you share it with your bookkeeper or payroll service so that they can prepare the employee's paycheck with the correct federal tax withholdings.

FICA Taxes

In addition to federal income tax withholdings, an employer has to withhold Social Security and Medicare taxes (referred to as FICA) from each employee's paycheck. FICA taxes are unique because they come in two parts: the required withholding from an employee's wages and an employer's portion of the tax.

BizFilings.com explains the FICA tax:

> The Federal Insurance Contributions Act (FICA) is the federal law that requires you to withhold three separate taxes from the wages you pay your employees. FICA is comprised of:
>
> - a 6.2 percent Social Security tax;
> - a 1.45 percent Medicare tax; and
> - 0.9 percent Medicare surtax when the employee earns over $200,000.
>
> You must withhold these amounts from an employee's wages.
>
> The law also requires you to pay the employer's portion of two of these taxes:
>
> - a 6.2 percent Social Security tax; and
> - a 1.45 percent Medicare tax (the "regular" Medicare tax).
>
> As you can see, the employer's portion for the Social Security tax and the regular Medicare tax is the same amount that you're required to withhold from your employees' wages. There is no employer portion for the 0.9 percent Medicare surtax on high-earning employees.
>
> In other words, you withhold a 6.2 percent Social Security tax from your employee's wages and you pay an additional 6.2 percent as your employer share of the tax (6.2 employee portion + 6.2 employer portion = 12.4 percent total). Also, you withhold a 1.45 percent Medicare tax from your employee's wages and you pay an additional 1.45 percent as your employer share (1.45 employee portion + 1.45 employer portion = 2.9 percent total). The total of all four portions is 15.3

percent (6.2 percent employee portion of Social Security + 6.2 percent employer portion of Social Security + 1.45 percent employee portion of Medicare + 1.45 percent employer portion of Medicare = 15.3 percent). [23]

SENDING IN YOUR EMPLOYER TAXES

Federal tax deposits (the periodic amounts you send in during the year to pay your employer taxes) must be made electronically, unless the small business exception applies. There are three methods that an employer can use to electronically transmit tax payments:

1. Use the Treasury Department's free Electronic Federal Tax Payment System (EFTPS).
2. Ask your bank to initiate an ACH (Automated Clearing House) credit payment on your behalf.
3. Use a bookkeeper, payroll service, or CPA with a payroll system to make the payment for you.

Small businesses with a federal tax liability of less than $2,500 per quarter can mail a check with their quarterly returns instead of making electronic payments. The check is mailed with a paper Form 941 Employer's Quarterly Federal Tax Return. See Chapter 7: Tax Forms for Employers for details on the Form 941.

Small businesses or nonprofits may be able to file a payroll tax return only once a year and not have to make deposits each quarter. If qualified (annual federal tax liability of $1,000 or less), small organizations can fill in Form 944 Employer's Annual Federal Tax Return and remit their tax payments with that return at the end of the year. More information on this annual Form 944 is covered in Chapter 7: Tax Forms for Employers.

STATE AND LOCAL PAYROLL TAX WITHHOLDINGS

It's not just your Uncle Sam that has tax withholding; your state and local government may also require income tax withholding. Most states use methods similar to the federal government in determining their state income tax withholding amounts. Most states have their own version of the federal Form W-4.

In some states there are cities, counties, and other local governmental units that impose their own income tax. If your employees work or live in one of these taxing localities, you need to withhold local tax as well as state and federal income tax. I had a tax client who paid a 1% city tax and then an additional 1.25% school tax. These taxpayers paid six taxes on the same income: federal income tax, state income tax, city income tax, school income tax, and of course Social Security and Medicare!

A helpful website of withholding requirements by state can be found at www.bizfilings.com/toolkit/sbg/tax-info/payroll-taxes/obligations.aspx.

EMPLOYER INSURANCE

Beyond employer taxes, there are required insurance programs that the federal government and most states require employers to purchase. These include unemployment coverage, workers compensation for on-the-job injuries and disability insurance for injuries away from work.

FEDERAL AND STATE UNEMPLOYMENT INSURANCE

You may have known about federal income tax withholding and FICA taxes if you've ever looked at a pay stub, but employers are also required to pay unemployment insurance premiums in the form of a tax to both their state and federal governments. These are known as SUTA and FUTA, respectively. These taxes are not withheld from the employee's pay. Instead they are paid in full by the employer.

Federal unemployment tax (FUTA) is a flat 0.6% on the first $7,000 in wages per employee. That would work out to be $42 per year per employee. State unemployment tax rates (also known as SUTA or SUI) are set by each state. They vary from 2% to 4% and are usually only on the first $7,000-$10,000 in wages per employee.

Some tax-exempt organizations are exempt from paying FUTA. If your homeschool organization has applied for and received 501(c)(3) tax-exempt status (you'll have a letter from the IRS to prove it), make sure your bookkeeper or payroll processor knows that you have 501(c)(3) status, so they do not have you filing a Form 940 and paying the FUTA tax.

Your 501(c)(3) organization is still liable for state unemployment taxes. But many states offer alternative programs to paying the SUTA. Called a reimbursing plan, a 501(c)(3) tax-exempt organization reimburses their state only for unemployment claims the state actually pays out to its former employees. Contact your state's unemployment agency to learn the details of alternative plans.

Worker's Compensation Insurance

FitsSmallBusiness.com offers some helpful information on Worker's Compensation insurance.

> Worker's compensation insurance covers claims by employees made against a business or nonprofit organization for job-related injuries or illness. With the exception of Texas, every state requires that you buy worker's compensation insurance. In most states, worker's compensation insurance is sold by private companies, although some states require you to buy it from specific state-managed carriers. This includes North Dakota, Ohio, Washington, and Wyoming.

> The cost of worker's compensation insurance varies tremendously, depending on your industry and location. For a tree trimmer, welder or road construction worker, the cost could be $15

per $100 in payroll, or higher. On the other hand, a banker, architect or attorney could pay under $0.25 per $100. So for an employee that earns $40,000 a year, a construction company may pay around $6,000, whereas a white collar business may pay just $100.

Additionally, after you've been in business for a while, your worker's compensation rates will go up or down depending on your accident history.

According to the National Academy of Social Insurance, the average small business pays about $1.50 per $100 in payroll for workers compensation insurance. [24]

Long and Short Term Disability Insurance

Disability insurance will pay an employee some portions of their income when they are ill or injured outside of their job. Worker's compensation insurance, discussed above, covers at-work injuries. Sometimes disability insurance is called paycheck insurance because it delivers a paycheck when a worker is unable to work. Short term disability (STD) coverage provides disabled employees with a percentage of their income—typically 60 percent—once sick leave is exhausted. Many of the conditions that trigger short term disability benefits include pregnancy, strains and sprains, and long illness.

Some states require employers buy short term (or temporary) disability insurance, but most do not require employers to provide this benefit. If your employees are located in any of the following states, you are required to purchase disability insurance:

- California: Employment Development Department at www.edd.ca.gov/Disability
- Hawaii: Disability Compensation Division at labor.hawaii.gov/dcd/
- New Jersey: Department of Labor and Workforce Development at lwd.dol.state.nj.us/labor/tdi/tdiindex.html

- New York: New York State Workers' Compensation Board at www.wcb.ny.gov/content/main/Employers/Employers.jsp
- Rhode Island: Department of Labor and Training at www.dlt.ri.gov/tdi/

Typical long term disability (LTD) benefits start when sick leave and short term benefits are exhausted, replace about 60 percent of pay, and continue anywhere from five years to the remainder of an individual's life. States and even the federal government have programs to replace income when a worker is disabled, but the payments are typically low and difficult to obtain. Many employers offer short and long term disabilities as a benefit to attract employees.

My daughter, Emily, broke her leg by slipping down a wet grassy hill in front of her apartment. Her employer's policy was for Emily to use her sick leave for the first two weeks she was off work. Then short term disability would pay her 60% of her salary for up to 6 more weeks. Emily was able to work from home (at full salary) after three weeks. She did not need to continue on short term disability and never needed long term disability. She was grateful her employer provided these benefits even though the state law did not require it.

Your homeschool organization should investigate the disability insurance laws if you have employees in the states listed above. Most states have an employer handbook on their websites. Look for exceptions based on the number of employees or exceptions for tax-exempt organizations. Consult an employee benefits specialist in your local area since laws and coverage vary by state. Start by asking several churches in your area who provides their employee insurance benefits.

Chapter 7: Tax Forms for Employers

This chapter introduces the forms employers use to report payroll and employer taxes to the Internal Revenue Service (IRS). I will not provide details explaining how to fill in these forms since they can vary widely depending on the type of employee (full-time, part-time) and the benefits you offer (vacation, sick days, retirement plans). My goal is to show these forms so that you are aware of what payroll forms your bookkeeper or payroll service should be filing. You (if you are the owner) or your organization's board members (if it is a nonprofit organization) are responsible for filing these forms, even if you hire a bookkeeper or payroll service. There are stiff penalties for failure to file these forms.

COMMON EMPLOYER FORMS

W-4 EMPLOYEE FEDERAL TAX WITHHOLDING

The Form W-4 Employee's Withholding Allowance Certificate is completed by each employee to tell the employer how much to withhold in federal income tax from the employee's pay. It is available online at IRS.gov. Employees can fill in a new W-4 every year or when their personal or financial situation changes and they desire to change their federal income tax withholdings.

Instructions on how to complete the Form W-4 are included on the form. If your employee needs help understanding the Form W-4, guide them to the internet for sources like TurboTax or this tutorial from Forbes writer, Taxgirl Kelly Erb tinyurl.com/KellyErbW4. In general, you can explain that the fewer allowances an employee claims, the more federal income tax will be withheld.

The employer does not send this form to the IRS. Instead, give a copy to your bookkeeper or payroll service. Retain W-4s for three years.

I-9 Employment Eligibility Verification

Unlike the other forms mentioned in this chapter, the Form I-9 is not an IRS form; the I-9 comes from the US Department of Homeland Security. It is used by an employer to verify an employee's identity and to establish that the worker is eligible to accept employment in the United States. Both the employee and the employer complete the Form I-9. Instructions are included on the form, which is available online at the US Citizens and Immigration website www.uscis.gov/sites/default/files/files/form/i-9.pdf. The Form I-9 is retained by the employer and not mailed to the government. Keep the I-9 for three years after hiring and one year after employment is ended. To learn more about Form I-9 visit www.uscis.gov/i-9-central.

W-2 Wage and Tax Statement

You may be quite familiar with the Form W-2 Wage and Tax Statement. It's the form that comes in late January every year to report wages earned and income tax withheld from the prior year. Your bookkeeper or payroll service will complete the Form W-2 and mail a copy to the employee. The employer also gets a copy and the third copy goes to the Social Security Administration (SSA), who shares it with the IRS.

22222	a Employee's social security number	OMB No. 1545-0008		
b Employer identification number (EIN)			1 Wages, tips, other compensation	2 Federal income tax withheld
c Employer's name, address, and ZIP code			3 Social security wages	4 Social security tax withheld
			5 Medicare wages and tips	6 Medicare tax withheld
			7 Social security tips	8 Allocated tips
d Control number			9	10 Dependent care benefits
e Employee's first name and initial Last name Suff.		11 Nonqualified plans	12a	
		13 Statutory employee Retirement plan Third-party sick pay	12b	
		14 Other	12c	
			12d	
f Employee's address and ZIP code				
15 State Employer's state ID number	16 State wages, tips, etc.	17 State income tax	18 Local wages, tips, etc.	19 Local income tax 20 Locality name

Form **W-2** Wage and Tax Statement 2016 Department of the Treasury—Internal Revenue Service
Copy 1—For State, City, or Local Tax Department

Employers must deliver W-2s and its related Form W-3 to all employees and to the SSA by January 31 each year. This is a change beginning in 2017. Employers used to have February 28 each year to submit the W-2s to the SSA. You can mail in paper versions of the W-2/W-3 or file online. Although you can see the Form W-2 online at www.irs.gov/pub/irs-pdf/fw2.pdf, you cannot print off the red-ink version of the Form W-2 Copy A. The IRS scanners cannot read your home-printed version. You can order copies of the red-ink version from the IRS or buy them at local office supply stores in December. I prefer filing the Forms W-2/W-3 online, which you can do directly with the SSA at www.ssa.gov/employer. There are also other online filing services. I use one called Yearli.com, which takes care of mailing copies to the employees and sending copies to the SSA.

The instructions for completing a W-2 are not included with the form. Instead the IRS offers a 32 page instruction guide to the Form W-2 and W-3 at www.irs.gov/pub/irs-pdf/iw2w3.pdf.

W-3 TRANSMITTAL OF WAGE AND TAX STATEMENTS

The Form W-3 is a cover sheet that accompanies your W-2s when submitting them to the Social Security Administration.

The W-3 is one of the simpler tax forms, since it is just a summary of all your W-2 forms, but alas it has the same pesky red ink, so your home-printed version is not acceptable to the IRS. You'll have to buy or order official red-ink versions or file online.

FORM 941 EMPLOYER'S QUARTERLY FEDERAL TAX RETURN

Employers who withhold income taxes, Social Security or Medicare tax from employees' paychecks and who must pay the employer's portion of Social Security and Medicare tax use Form 941 to report these taxes. This two-page form is completed each quarter and includes a payment voucher for the employer to send in a payment for employer taxes.

The Form is available on line at www.irs.gov/pub/irs-pdf/f941.pdf. Instructions can be found at www.irs.gov/pub/irs-pdf/i941.pdf. If you use a payroll service they will prepare the Form 941 for you each quarter. These forms can be mailed to the IRS or electronically filed using a service like Yearli.com or any IRS-approved providers. Find IRS-approved e-filing services by going to IRS.gov and searching on "approved modernized e-File." Then select "94x e-file."

Form 944 Employer's Annual Federal Tax Return

Small employers whose annual liability for Social Security, Medicare, and withheld federal income taxes is $1,000 or less can file a Form 944 and pay these taxes only once a year instead of every quarter.

The IRS will notify you if you are eligible to file the Form 944. If you haven't received notification to file Form 944 but estimate that your employment tax liability for a calendar year will be $1,000 or less and would like to file Form 944 instead of Forms 941, you can contact the IRS to request to file Form 944. You must call the IRS at 1-800-829-4933 or 267-941-1000 (toll call) before April 1 to request permission to file Form 944.

This annual report may be an option for small homeschool organizations with total annual payroll of about $4,000-$6,000. Work closely with your bookkeeper, accountant, or payroll service to determine if your homeschool organization is eligible to use Form 944 and only file and pay employer taxes once a year.

Form 940 Employer's Annual Federal Unemployment (FUTA) Tax Return

The Form 940 is used to report your annual Federal Unemployment Tax Act (FUTA) tax. Yes, there are more taxes than federal income tax, Social Security and Medicare tax, but we're nearly finished! The FUTA tax provides funds for paying unemployment compensation to workers who have lost their jobs. Most employers pay both a federal and a state unemployment tax. Only employers pay FUTA tax; employees do not pay the FUTA tax. Do not collect or deduct FUTA tax from your employees' wages.

The Form 940 is available online at www.irs.gov/pub/irs-pdf/f940.pdf. Its instructions are available at www.irs.gov/pub/irs-pdf/i940.pdf. The due date for filing the Form 940 is February 1 for the previous year's tax. You can pay all your FUTA tax once in January if you owe $500 or less. If you will owe more than $500, then you should make quarterly payments throughout the year. Work closely with your payroll service to submit the FUTA tax correctly.

Here's some good news: 501(c)(3) tax-exempt organizations do not have to pay FUTA tax nor file the Form 940! The instructions to the Form 940 state this:

> Religious, educational, scientific, charitable, and other organizations described in section 501(c)(3) and exempt from tax under section 501(a) aren't subject to FUTA tax and don't have to file Form 940.[25]

STATE EMPLOYER TAX FORMS

As if these federal forms are not enough, each state has its own employer forms as well. For example, in Ohio there is a state income tax reporting form similar to the Form 941. It is filed quarterly. There is also a state unemployment tax with quarterly filings and worker's compensation which is filed semi-annually. Ohio allows each of its 88 counties and cities to levy local income tax and school tax. These are withheld from employees' wages and submitted by the employer.

I am not going to cover all the state employer reporting forms in this book. It wouldn't be practical or easy to lift! I advise you to visit your state department of revenue website. Look for information on employers' taxes. Intuit (makers of QuickBooks) has compiled a list of state tax agencies for you at payroll.intuit.com/state_agencies/.

I think you've probably read all you care to read about federal and state employer taxes. You may be confused, frustrated, and overwhelmed at the thought of preparing payroll forms. Not to fear, there are people willing to do payroll for you, and I strongly recommend you hire a bookkeeper or payroll service so you can focus on running your homeschool program. Leave payroll taxes to the experienced experts.

Chapter 8: Sample Independent Contractor Agreements

In this chapter, I offer several independent contractor agreements. Explanatory notes are in italics and should be deleted from the final agreement with your independent contractor.

I also recommend you search the Internet for sample independent contractor agreements that fit your organization. It is usually advisable to have an attorney review your agreement and offer suggestions. These samples may be modified to fit your unique needs and do not constitute giving legal advice or an opinion.

INDEPENDENT CONTRACTOR AGREEMENT FOR TUTOR OR TEACHER

This agreement is short enough to cover almost everything needed. It does not mention who is responsible for securing a substitute teacher, nor does it mention that the independent contractor must provide her own tools and equipment. You may wish to add those provisions.

This agreement is made and entered into as of this _____ day of ____, _____, by and between _____(contractor's name), the Contractor and _____(organization's name), the Organization.

_____(contractor's name) is considered to be an independent contractor providing educational services to the Organization and as such shall be responsible for reporting all compensation to the IRS, state, and city tax agencies. Additionally, no federal, state or city income taxes will be withheld from contractor's compensation.

The Contractor agrees to provide the Organization with a completed IRS Form W-9. The information on the W-9 is needed for the Organization to fulfill its legal reporting requirements to the IRS. Compensation will not be given until the contractor has provided the Organization with a fully completed and signed Form W-9.

1.) Independent Contractor Services

In consideration of the mutual promises and covenants contained herein, and for other good and valuable consideration, the receipt and sufficiency of which is hereby acknowledged, the parties hereto agree as follows:

- Contractor shall provide _____ weeks/days/hours of educational services.

  or

Contractor shall teach _____ *(class name)* for _____ *(time period such as Spring semester 20xx).*

- Contractor shall diligently and competently perform duties of class teacher.
- Contractor shall be respectful, cooperative, and civil with parents/guardians, students, board members, staff, and other independent contractors at all times.

Add additional requirements or description of the assignment if desired.

2.) Contract term

The term of the Contractor's services shall commence on _____and shall terminate on _____; unless sooner terminated by either party as provided in this agreement.

3.) Compensation.

In full consideration for the performance of the Services hereunder, the Organization shall pay the Contractor as follows (check as applicable):

_____ on a time and materials basis at the following rates: _____.

or

_____ a fixed fee in the amount of $ _____ payable in installments as follows: _____.

Payments shall be preceded by an invoice from the Contractor (to be submitted monthly), which Organization shall then pay in the ordinary course.

(optional) The Organization will reimburse the Contractor for reasonable and necessary expenses incurred in the performance of the Services. All such expenses shall be subject to the Organization's prior approval.

Contractor acknowledges and agrees that it shall not be entitled to, and the Organization shall not be obligated to pay, any monies or other compensation for the Services provided under this Agreement.

4.) Termination of contract

This contract may be terminated by Contractor at any time upon giving the Organization ____ days of written notice of intent to do so. The Organization may terminate this contract upon any breach of this Agreement or any other good cause (such as classes not filling or space considerations) or upon the dissolving of the Organization for any reason.

5.) Payments to Contractor upon termination of contract

In the event of the termination of the Contractor's contract pursuant to section # 4 above, Contractor shall be entitled to any compensation as described in section # 3 above and accrued up to the effective date of termination. If the termination was due to the death of the Contractor, such accrued compensation shall be paid to her/his Executor or Administrator or, if no Executor/Administrator has been appointed, then to a personal representative or heir.

6.) Limitation of authority

Contractor shall have no right or authority to bind or otherwise legally commit the Organization, families, or members on any contract, promise, or other commitment, whether oral or written.

7.) Contract renewal option

This agreement shall automatically expire on _____ without any further action or notice required by either party. Any subsequent contract for the following program year shall be conditioned upon the execution of and subject to the terms and conditions of a new written agreement by the parties hereto.

The contractor shall confirm her/his desire to continue offering services to the Organization by _____(date).

8.) Entire agreement

This agreement contains the entire agreement of the parties and fully supersedes any and all prior agreements or understandings, whether oral or written.

9.) Modification and waiver

No alteration of, or modification to, any of the provisions of this agreement shall be valid unless made in writing and signed by both parties. The waiver by any party of a breach of any provision of this Agreement by the other party shall not operate or be construed as a waiver of any subsequent breach by such party.

IN WITNESS WHEREOF, the parties hereto have executed this Agreement:

_____   _____
Organization Representative   Independent Contractor

LONGER INDEPENDENT CONTRACTOR AGREEMENT

This agreement is quite long and uses more formal language. It can be used for a variety of independent contractor tasks, not just teaching a class. It uses three attachments (called Exhibits): a Form W-9, a description of the contracted services, and a liability waiver. You may not want such a long contract, but may like the structure (using attachments) and find some of the provisions useful in your independent contractor agreement.

INDEPENDENT CONTRACTOR AGREEMENT

C-- HOMESCHOOL COMMUNITY, INC., (herein after "CHC"), and _____, an individual, (hereinafter "Contractor") hereby enter into this agreement (this "Agreement") on this _____ day of _____, 20__, pursuant to which Contractor agrees to furnish certain services and/or work product specified in this Agreement under the terms and conditions and for the consideration set forth herein.

1. <u>Contractor Status and Obligations.</u>

   a. Contractor agrees to furnish to CHC the services and/or work product (hereinafter collectively referred to as "Contractor Services") described on Exhibit A attached hereto and made a part hereof by this reference (hereinafter, "Exhibit A"). Contractor is furnishing the Contractor Services under this Agreement as an independent contractor and will be solely responsible for all federal, state and local tax obligations imposed with respect to payments received from CHC.

   b. Upon execution of this Agreement, Contractor will provide to CHC a completed W-9 form (in the form of Exhibit A, attached hereto and made a part hereof by this reference "Exhibit A").

   c. CHC and Contractor acknowledge and agree that CHC will not pay any Federal Insurance Contribution Act ("FICA"), Social Security contribution, Medicare contribution, Federal Unemployment Tax Act ("FUTA"), or state unemployment or withholding taxes, nor will CHC withhold any pay on Contractor's account regarding any income tax withholding or FICA, FUTA, or state unemployment taxes.

   d. CHC will not cover Contractor or its employees for Worker's Compensation purposes.

   e. Neither Contractor, nor any of its employees, shall be entitled to receive any benefits which CHC's employees, if any, may be entitled to receive, including but not limited to medical insurance, life insurance, paid vacation, paid holidays, pension, or profit sharing.

2. Services and/or Work Product to be Furnished: CHC hereby engages Contractor to furnish the Contractor Services described on Exhibit B. Contractor hereby agrees to furnish the Contractor Services pursuant to the terms of Exhibit B and this Agreement.

3. Contractor Fee and Payment Terms: CHC hereby agrees to pay Contractor the amount listed on Exhibit B as the contractor fee ("Contractor Fee"). Payment shall be made in full on the Contractor Fee Payment Date, identified on Exhibit B (the "Contractor Fee Payment Date"). Contractor hereby agrees to accept the Contractor Fee as payment in full for the Contractor Services and to sign such receipts and affidavits as CHC shall reasonably request in order to acknowledge payment.

4. Instructions and Training: CHC will provide no instructions or training to Contractor with respect to the Contractor Services. While CHC will provide to Contractor the specifications with which the Contractor Services must comply, Contractor retains full independence in exercising its judgment regarding the time, means, and manner by which it performs the Contractor Service.

5. Expenses: Contractor shall be solely responsible for all expenses incurred and shall furnish any tools, equipment, and materials necessary in connection with provision of Contractor Service. Contractor will not have any rights of reimbursement against CHC for any expenditures pertaining thereto.

6. Risk: Contractor shall perform the Contractor Services and its work toward fulfillment of its duties under this Agreement at its own risk, including, but not limited to, responsibility for condition of tools, equipment, transportation, and materials. Contractor hereby agrees to indemnify and hold harmless CHC and --- Church, its employees, agents, and assigns from any claim, demand, loss, liability, damage, or expense of any sort arising in any way from Contractor's performance of its duties under this Agreement. Within ten (10) days of request by CHC, Contractor shall provide proof of liability insurance deemed adequate by CHC in its sole discretion.

   It is not typical for homeschool contractors, especially if they are homeschool parents teaching in a homeschool co-op, to have liability insurance. Your organization may wish to exclude this provision.

   Notwithstanding anything to the contrary set forth in this paragraph, except for acts of negligence or willful misconduct, Contractor shall not be liable for accident or injury occurring before, during or after any activity in which students (of CHC or other) are engaged while on Church's premises.

7. Assignment: CHC may assign any or all of its rights and duties under this Agreement at any time and from time to time without the consent of Contractor. Contractor retains discretion regarding the use of employees and assistants in the execution of its duties under this Agreement, provided, however, that:
   a. CHC has not specifically prohibited the use of certain individuals or corporations to which CHC has a reasonable objection; and

b. Contractor is responsible for all compensation owed such individuals. Contractor shall hold CHC harmless with respect to liability for any amounts owed to or regarding such individuals. Irrespective of whether Contractor engages such individuals, Contractor retains full responsibility for all duties, liabilities, and any obligations of any nature, whatsoever, for which Contractor is responsible by virtue of its entering into this Agreement.

> *This provision is rather passive in regards to the homeschool organization approving substitutes. It states that the independent contractor can chose employees and assistants so long as CHC doesn't object. Some homeschool groups many want to consider requiring any substitutes be officially approved by the homeschool organization.*

8. <u>Term</u>: This Agreement is effective as of the date first above written and shall continue in effect until the termination date listed on Exhibit B (the "Termination Date"), unless cancelled by CHC for reasonable cause upon prior written notice to Contractor. This Agreement shall not create or imply any other sort of ongoing relationship between CHC and Contractor, except with respect to the Contractor Services described herein. Following the Termination Date, this Agreement shall continue in effect only so long as, and to the extent, required to govern any rights and duties of either party created by this Agreement which naturally survive the furnishing of Contractor Services.

9. <u>Choice of Law:</u> This Agreement shall be governed by the laws of the State of XXX, and the only venue of legal action hereunder shall be the Circuit Court for the County of XXX County, XXX.

10. <u>Agreement Supersedes Any Previous Agreement</u>: This Agreement is intended to supersede and replace any and all previous agreement, either oral or written, between the parties hereto, including any and all amendments thereto.

11. <u>Modifications:</u> No modification, amendment, or change to this Agreement shall be binding on CHC or on Contractor unless and until same shall have been approved in writing by both parties. This Agreement constitutes the entire agreement between CHC and Contractor.

12. <u>Severability</u>: If any provisions of this Agreement shall be held invalid or unenforceable for any reason, then such invalidity or unenforceability shall not affect any other part of this Agreement, and the parts of this Agreement not invalid or unenforceable shall remain in full force and effect.

13. <u>Waiver.</u> Failure to invoke any right, condition, or covenant in this Agreement by either party shall not be deemed to imply or constitute a waiver of any rights, condition, or covenant and neither party may rely on such failure. Contractor and each of its employees, agents or assigns who perform Contractor Services under this Agreement shall execute a Waiver and Release in the form attached hereto as Exhibit C (hereinafter, "Exhibit C".)

14. <u>Binding.</u> This Agreement shall not be binding until CHC and Contractor have both executed the Agreement and all exhibits.

15. <u>Notice.</u> Any notice or communication permitted or required by this Agreement shall be deemed effective when personally delivered or deposited, postage prepaid, in the first class mail of the United States properly addressed to the appropriate party at the address provided.

    Many homeschool organizations prefer the speed of email rather than physical mail. Add your email address if you agree to communicate that way with your contractors.

16. <u>Inclement Weather.</u> In the event of inclement weather, CHC will follow the XXX County School System's closing policy. If CHC is cancelled due to weather, Contractor and CHC shall make every

reasonable effort to reschedule Contractor's classes at a mutually agreeable time and location.

IN WITNESS WHEREOF, the parties hereto have executed this Agreement the day and year first above written.

EXHIBIT A
W-9 Form filled in by Contractor *(not shown here).*

EXHIBIT B
This Exhibit B is attached to that certain Independent Contractor Agreement dated _____, 20__ (the "Agreement"), made between C---HOMESCHOOL COMMUNITY, INC., a STATE corporation ("CHC"), and _____ (hereinafter, "Contractor").

The defined terms in this Exhibit B shall have the same meanings ascribed to such terms in the Agreement.

NOW, THEREFORE, CHC and Contractor do hereby agree:

1.   CONTRACTOR SERVICES: Contractor hereby agrees to provide appropriate instruction to the students during the CHC's Homeschool Co-op Program (the Co-op):

2.   CLASS DATES: Contractor will perform the Contractor Services during the Co-op's meetings at XXX Church on the following the Co-op's dates and times:

The last day of the Co-op's meeting _____, 20__ is hereinafter referred to as Termination Date".

3.   CONTRACTOR FEE: Contractor will perform the Contractor Services during the Co-op's meetings in consideration of the Contractor Fee in the amount of _____DOLLARS ($____).

The Contractor Fee represents is _____ Dollars ($___) per student for the entire Co-op session, multiplied by the number of students in Contractor's class.

This co-op explains how the total fee is calculated (a set rate multiplied by the number of students in class). Some homeschool organizations may choose not to disclose the rate or calculation, but simply state the full amount to be paid.

4. CONTRACTOR FEE PAYMENT DATE: CHC shall pay Contractor the Contractor Fee by check on _____, 20__ (the last day of the Co-op's session).

This co-op pays in full on the last day of the Co-op session. That is not typical because most contractors prefer some sort of progress payment such as payment in monthly allotments.

5. SUPPLIES, MATERIAL, EQUIPMENT: At its own expense, Contractor shall supply, and Contractor's Fee includes reimbursement for, all supplies, materials, and equipment required to render Contractor's Services, including, but not limited to, the following: necessary scripts, props, costumes, and office supplies.

IN WITNESS WHEREOF, the parties hereto have executed this Agreement the day and year first above written.

EXHIBIT C

WAIVER AND RELEASE *(not included here)*

Short and Sweet Independent Contractor Agreement

Teacher Agreement with XXX Homeschool Cooperative for _____ *(year)*

Teacher Name: _____

Service(s) provided: _____

Compensation for the School Year payable in ___ monthly install-ments, beginning _____ *(date)*: \$_____ /month *(or total amount)*

Dates: _____ School Year (on or about ____ through ___)

_____I agree to support the mission and Statement of Faith of XXX Homeschool Co-op and to perform the duties I have been assigned in a professional manner and in compliance with any rules, regulations, and requirements set forth in the XXX Homeschool Co-op Family Handbook.

_____I agree that I will show up on time and be fully prepared to per-form the duties I have been assigned.

_____I understand that if I miss more than 2 days of class this agree-ment may be terminated.

_____I agree to submit to a background check, at the expense of XXX Homeschool Co-op, no later than _____ *(date)*. I understand that a criminal history record acceptable to the XXX Homeschool Co-op at its sole discretion is a condition of this Contract.

_____I agree that if I wish to terminate my position I must give ___ days notice.

_____I agree that all curricula, lesson plans, weekly assignment sheets, and supplies are property of XXX Homeschool Co-op and may not be distributed to anyone other than XXX Homeschool Co-op members, and must be returned to XXX Homeschool Co-op at the end of the _____ school year or upon exiting the program.

_____I agree to maintain appropriate confidentiality with regard to teacher, student, parent and co-op matters. I will not gossip or involve volunteers, parents or others. If I have concerns about a student or situation, I will direct them to the XXX Homeschool Co-op Director or Board of Directors.

_____   _____

Signature   Date

_____   _____

Homeschool Co-op   Date
Director Signature

INDEPENDENT CONTRACTOR AGREEMENT FOR BOOKKEEPER OR OTHER VENDOR

This is a sample agreement I have used in the past to offer my bookkeeping services to a client. It comes from the perspective of the independent contractor. If you hire a bookkeeper, graphic designer or website designer, they may have a standard agreement they use.

AGREEMENT OF PROFESSIONAL SERVICES BETWEEN INDEPENDENT CONTRACTOR AND HOMESCHOOL ORGANIZATION

Services to be rendered

General bookkeeping services including:

- Receive banking and financial transactions from Homeschool organization's bank either from statements or on-line downloads
- Record transactions in accounting software
- Monthly bank reconciliation
- Maintain financial records
- Report periodically (monthly or quarterly) income and expenses
- Additional services such as payroll or contractor payments or budgeting can be negotiated separately.

Limitations

Contractor is not responsible for bill payments or tax payments.

Contractor is not authorized to sign checks or make payments.

Contractor is not authorized to make on-line bank transfers, deposits or payments to myself or third parties.

Fees and payment:

Contractor will charge $___ per hour. Estimated total time will be ___ to ____ hours a month, but this varies with the amount of activity in the Homeschool Organization.

Contractor will invoice Homeschool Organization on a monthly basis, and payment will be due two weeks after receipt of the invoice.

Liabilities and Responsibilities: The maximum amount of Contractor liability exposure is the amount of Contractor's fees. Contractor is not liable for harm caused by Homeschool Organization's failure to perform a needed task or disclose pertinent information. The accuracy of financial information supplied to Contractor is the sole responsibility of the Homeschool Organization. Contractor shall not be held responsible for the production of inaccurate financial statements, or any other financial reports if the financial data submitted by Homeschool Organization is inaccurate.

Homeschool Organization understands and agrees that some of the data entry may be performed by assistants hired by Contractor to perform data entry.

Confidentiality: Contractor acknowledges that Homeschool Organization has confidential and personal information and will not disclose personal or business information to any third party. Contractor will safe guard Homeschool Organization's information with passwords and physical security measures at Contractor's office.

Signed:

_____   _____
Contractor   date

_____   _____
Homeschool Organization   date

Speaker Agreement

This is an agreement I have sent to agree to be a speaker at a home-school event.

Speaker Agreement between ____ (event host) and _____ (speaker)

Dear (Speaker Name):

We, the event host, are delighted to be working with you. This letter will serve as a confirmation of our conversation and as a letter of agreement. You, the speaker, will speak to our group according to the following details:

Organization:

Event leader's name:

    Phone:

    Email:

Presentation Topic/Title:

Presentation Date:

Location:

Address:

Booking Terms and Conditions:

Speaker agrees to present to the best of your ability the information described above. Speaker agrees to coordinate the details of this program with the event host in order to achieve the outcomes that we have stated.

We (event host) agree to:
- duplicate the handouts provided by the speaker
- allow the speaker to sell books and CDs at the event

- provide a complementary table/booth
- provide the room setup
- provide audiovisual equipment including projector and screen, if needed
- arrange lodging, if needed
- reimburse for meals
- reimburse travel expenses by car or air
- to compensate as follows:

Travel Expenses Details (if required):

Round trip travel from _____: $.55/mile or coach class airfare in North America.

Ground transportation or rental car if traveling by air.

Hotel accommodations: Event host will reserve a non-smoking, pet-free room, with late check-out approved, and late arrival guaranteed.

Meals: Event host will reimburse all speaker meal expenses or provide meals while traveling and day(s) of presentation. Event host agrees to reimburse all speaker meal expenses within 30 days of receipt of your invoice.

Speaker Honorarium: See attached fee schedule.

Total Fee Payable: $_____

Please make checks payable to _____ (speaker or business name).

The speaking fee is due the date of the presentation. Event host agrees to pay all travel and meal reimbursements within 30 days of receipt of your invoice.

Postponement/Cancellation:

If either party is forced to cancel this contract due to illness, accident, or natural disaster, neither party, nor any representative shall be liable for any payment of speaking fees. 100% reimbursement of nonrefundable airfare fees will be paid by event host. If this event is postponed or canceled the following schedule will apply from the time written notification is received by the speaker:

- Less than 7 days before: 50% of speaking fee will be paid to speaker. 100% reimbursement of nonrefundable airfare fees will be paid to speaker.
- Between 7 - 30 days before: 25% of speaking fee will be paid to speaker. 100% reimbursement of nonrefundable airfare fees will be paid to speaker.
- More than 30 days: no speaking fee will be charged. 100% reimbursement of nonrefundable airfare fees will be paid to speaker.

The event host agrees not to audio or video tape the presentation without prior written permission of the speaker.

This constitutes the entire agreement between the parties.

Event Host: _____ Date:_____

Speaker: _____ Date: _____

Chapter 9: Resources

This chapter includes lists resources mentioned in previous chapters as well as additional books, videos, and websites you may find helpful.

WORKER CLASSIFICATION DETERMINATION

Carol Topp, CPA will conduct a fact-based analysis of your relationship with your workers to determine their proper worker classification. Her determination will be provided to you in writing and will be accompanied with a letter explaining the consequences of misclassification and recommendations to follow. Visit HomeschoolCPA.com/Services for details and fees.

MANAGING A HOMESCHOOL ORGANIZATION

Homeschool Co-ops: How to Start Them, Run Them and Not Burn Out has by Carol Topp, CPA.

Money Management in a Homeschool Organization: A Guide for Treasurers by Carol Topp, CPA.

The IRS and Your Homeschool Organization: Tax Exempt Status for Homeschool Organizations by Carol Topp, CPA.

All books available at HomeschoolCPA.com/Bookstore.

HIRING INDEPENDENT CONTRACTORS

IRS Publication 1779 *Independent Contractor or Employee* www.irs.gov/pub/irs-pdf/p1779.pdf.

Nolo.com, the publisher of helpful business books, has an online fill-in independent contractor agreement. You can pick options to customize the agreement. The fee is $29 a year. Available at: www.nolo.com/products/contract-with-independent-contractor-noe3-pr113.html

PAYROLL SERVICES

To find a payroll service, start with your local bank. Many banks are offering payroll services. These may be only software that you can use to prepare payroll yourself, or they may be able to recommend a full-featured payroll service. If you are a nonprofit organization, ask your local bank if they have a discounted rate for nonprofits.

Intuit Payroll. If you are using QuickBooks for your accounting software, you can add on a payroll service. Several levels are available starting at $20 per month for do-it-yourself payroll. You can even use Intuit Payroll if you don't use QuickBooks. payroll.intuit.com.

Square Payroll. I love my Square reader that lets me accept credit cards using my iPhone, and so I was excited to learn about Square Payroll. As of this book's publication date the fee is $20 per month plus $5 per employee and is available in a limited number of states. squareup.com/payroll.

OnPay charges $40 per month for up to 10 employees. This may work well for small homeschool organizations with just a few employees. www.payrollcenter.com/onpay/index.html.

Surepayroll.com Fill in their questionnaire for a quote.

Flashpayroll.com Email them for a quote.

Gusto.com might be a good option if your organization has one employee and several contractors.

Doing Manual Payroll

Intuit is the creator of QuickBooks. Their chart of options shows the advantages and tradeoffs of manual payroll or using a payroll service. payroll.intuit.com/resources/learn-payroll.

Intuit also offers a free ebook *Highlights from Hire Your First Employee* http-download.intuit.com/http.intuit/CMO/payments/general-pdfs/Hire_Mini_Guide.pdf.

"Employer's Tax Guide: Publication 15, Circular E" –Internal Revenue Service. Available at: www.irs.gov/publications/p15/index.html.

FitsSmallBusiness.com has a resources page "Payroll Basics: How To Pay Employees Resources" at fitsmallbusiness.com/payroll-basics-how-to-pay-resources.

Payroll Management: 2016 Edition by Steven M. Bragg. There are chapters dealing with payroll accounting and how to set up a system of procedures, controls, and record keeping. This book is written for bookkeepers or accountants by a CPA. It is very detailed, but if you have someone willing to learn how to do payroll, this would be helpful.

YouTube has dozens of videos on preparing payroll. Start by searching on "Payroll with QuickBooks" or "Do It Yourself Payroll" or "Payroll with Excel" depending on your interest.

LEGAL ASPECTS OF HIRING EMPLOYEES

"Do I have to Comply with the Fair Labor Standards Act?"–United States Department of Labor. Available at: www.dol.gov/elaws/esa/flsa/scope/screen24.asp.

Hiring Your First Employee: A Step-by-Step Guide by Attorney Fred S. Steingold. This book covers anti-discrimination laws, responsibilities of a business owner when they hire an employee (insurance, taxes, etc.), employment at will, hiring and firing and much, more.

The Employer's Legal Handbook: Manage Your Employees & Workplace Effectively by Fred S. Steingold. The same author of the book listed above is an attorney and focuses on workplace laws and regulations.

Essential Guide to Federal Employment Laws 5th Edition by Lisa Guerin J.D. Use the Amazon Look Inside to read the chart of various employment laws.

The Nonprofit Hiring Toolkit offered by Bridgespan.org, a global nonprofit, includes tips on legal and illegal interview questions: www.bridgespan.org/Publications-and-Tools/Hiring-Nonprofit-Leaders/Nonprofit-Hiring-Toolkit.aspx. Note: Religious organizations may discriminate on the basis of religious beliefs if the practice and promotion of the religion is part of their tax-exempt purpose.

Payroll Tax Obligations

BizFilings.com has several webpages devoted to payroll obligations including:

Payroll taxes overview: www.bizfilings.com/toolkit/sbg/tax-info/payroll-taxes.aspx

Payroll taxes that apply to employees: www.bizfilings.com/toolkit/sbg/tax-info/payroll-taxes/determining-payroll-taxes-for-employees.aspx

State and local taxes: www.bizfilings.com/toolkit/sbg/tax-info/payroll-taxes/employee-state-and-local-payroll-tax-obligations.aspx

Income tax withholding obligations by state: www.bizfilings.com/toolkit/sbg/tax-info/payroll-taxes/obligations.aspx

Create an Employee Handbook

Download a template for an employee handbook at www.nonprofithr.com/portfolio/essential-nonprofit-employee-handbook-template.

Internal Revenue Service Publications

IRS Publication 3079 Tax-*exempt Organizations and Gaming,* has a helpful section titled, "Volunteer Labor." www.irs.gov/pub/irs-pdf/p3079.pdf.

IRS Publication 1779 *Independent Contractor or Employee* www.irs.gov/pub/irs-pdf/p1779.pdf.

Internal Revenue Service Forms

IRS Form SS-8 Form 1099-MISC Determination of Worker Status for Purposes of Federal Employment Taxes and Income Tax Withholding. www.irs.gov/pub/irs-pdf/fss8.pdf.

IRS Form 1096 Annual Summary and Transmittal of U.S. Information Returns. www.irs.gov/pub/irs-pdf/f1096.pdf.

Form W-4 Employee's Withholding Allowance Certificate www.irs.gov/pub/irs-pdf/fw4.pdf

W-2 Wage and Tax Statement www.irs.gov/pub/irs-pdf/fw2.pdf.

W-3 Transmittal of Wage and Tax Statements www.irs.gov/pub/irs-pdf/fw3.pdf.

Instruction guide to the Form W-2 and W-3 at www.irs.gov/pub/irs-pdf/iw2w3.pdf.

Form 941 Employer's Quarterly Federal Tax Return. The Form is available on line at www.irs.gov/pub/irs-pdf/f941.pdf. Instructions can be found at www.irs.gov/pub/irs-pdf/i941.pdf.

Form 944 Employer's Annual Federal Tax Return. The Form is available on line at www.irs.gov/pub/irs-pdf/f944.pdf. Instructions can be found at www.irs.gov/pub/irs-pdf/i944.pdf.

Form 940 Employer's Annual Federal Unemployment (FUTA) Tax Return. The Form 940 is available online at www.irs.gov/pub/irs-pdf/f940.pdf. Its instructions are available at www.irs.gov/pub/irs-pdf/i940.pdf.

CONFLICT OF INTEREST POLICY

The Board Cafe website from CompassPoint.org offers a sample Conflict of Interest policy at www.compasspoint.org/board-cafe/sample-conflict-interest-policy.

A sample conflict of interest policy from NonProfitRisk.org opens as a Microsoft Word document: www.nonprofitrisk.org/advice/samples/ConflictPolicy.doc.

About the Author

Carol L. Topp, CPA, is an accountant and a retired homeschooling mother. She earned her Bachelor of Science degree from Purdue University and worked as a Cost Analyst for the US Navy for ten years. In 2000, Carol passed the Certified Public Accountant (CPA) examination. Carol began homeschooling her two daughters when they started first grade. They are now homeschool high school graduates (and college graduates!). She was very active in her local homeschool community teaching classes and speaking at support group meetings.

As an accountant, Carol has served on several not-for-profit boards. She has consulted with leaders from over 300 homeschool organizations and helped more than 80 organizations obtain 501(c)(3) tax-exempt status. In addition, Carol prepares the annual Form 990 reporting with the Internal Revenue Service (IRS) for several homeschool and nonprofit groups. In 2006, Carol launched her website www.HomeschoolCPA.com to help homeschool organizations lead successful groups. It was voted a Top Accounting Blog in 2015.

She is the author of *Homeschool Co-ops: How to Start Them, Run Them and Not Burn Out, The IRS and Your Homeschool Organization, Money Management in a Homeschool Organization: A Guide for Treasurers* and *Paying Workers in a Homeschool Organization.*

Carol's publications include numerous articles, podcasts and webinars about operating a homeschool nonprofit organization. Her articles have appeared in *The Old Schoolhouse, Home Education* and *Home School Enrichment* magazines. In addition, Carol has enjoyed conducting workshops for homeschool leaders at conventions across the country.

As a professional accountant, Carol's affiliations include the Ohio Society of CPAs, the National Association of Tax Professionals, and the Ohio Society of CPAs Speakers Bureau.

Carol lives with her husband in Cincinnati, Ohio, where she enjoys reading, painting, traveling, and helping homeschool leaders.

Carol can be contacted through her website www.HomeschoolCPA.com.

If you found *Paying Workers in a Homeschool Organization* helpful, visit HomeschoolCPA.com for other books by Carol Topp, CPA including:

Homeschool Co-ops: How to Start Them, Run Them and Not Burn Out

The IRS and Your Homeschool Organization

Money Management in a Homeschool Organization: A Guide for Treasurers

Visit **HomeschoolCPA.com** for more information on starting a running a homeschool organization.

Worker Classification Determination For Homeschool Organizations

- Is your homeschool teacher an employee or independent contractor?
- Should your homeschool co-op director be paid as an employee?
- How difficult is it to set up a payroll system?
- What happens if my homeschool group misclassifies a worker?

Worker classification can be a confusing topic.

This book *Paying Workers in a Homeschool Organization* can help clear a lot of confusion, but perhaps you want to discuss your particular situation in a private, individual phone consultation.

Carol Topp, CPA offers a service to help you determine if your homeschool organization's workers are employees or independent contractors. The service will include a phone interview and will be followed up with Carol's determination in writing, recommendations of changes you should make, and the consequences of misclassification.

To request a consultation, visit HomeschoolCPA.com/Services.

Index

All websites URLs were accurate as of September 10, 2016

Notes

1 "De Minimis Fringe Benefits." www.irs.gov/government-enti-ties/federal-state-local-governments/de-minimis-fringe-benefits

2 "Eight Tips to Determine if Your Gift is Taxable" www.irs.gov/uac/eight-tips-to-determine-if-your-gift-is-taxable

3 Ibid.

4 Hammar, Richard r., "How Do We Report Gifts Provided to Volunteers?" Church Treasurer Alert, December 2007 nsrba.org/clienti-mages/20851/how%20do%20we%20report%20gifts%20provided%20to%20volunteers-2.pdf

5 Instructions for Form 1023 www.irs.gov/instructions/i1023/ch02.html#d0e1909

6 "Reasonable Compensation," 1993 EO CPE text www.irs.gov/pub/irs-tege/eotopici93.pdf

7 "Exempt Organizations: Compensation of Officers" www.irs.gov/charities-non-profits/exempt-organizations-compensation-of-officers

8 "Should Board Members of Nonprofit Organizations Be Compensated?" *ASAE*, www.asaecenter.org/resources/articles/an_plus/2015/december/should-board-members-of-nonprofit-organizations-be-compensated

9 26 U.S. Code § 117 - Qualified scholarships: www.law.cornell.edu/cfr/text/26/1.170A-9

10 Behavioral Control www.irs.gov/Businesses/Small-Businesses-&-Self-Employed/Behavioral-Control

11 Ibid.

12 Ibid.

13 Financial Control www.irs.gov/businesses/small-businesses-self-employed/financial-control

14 Type of Relationship. www.irs.gov/Businesses/Small-Businesses-&-Self-Employed/Type-of-Relationship

15 Exempt Organizations Workshop Participant Text. Training 4325-002 (Rev 7-2010) Catalog Number 88908P. Department of Treasury. Internal Revenue Service.

16 Type of Relationship. www.irs.gov/Businesses/Small-Businesses-&-Self-Employed/Type-of-Relationship

17 "Independent Contractor (Self-Employed) or Employee?" https://www.irs.gov/businesses/small-businesses-self-employed/independent-contractor-self-employed-or-employee

18 "Focus on Nonprofit Employee Misclassification" *Venable LLP,* www.venable.com/files/Event/624c3096-6e46-4d2c-8fdc-a674c30ad5f0/Presentation/EventAttachment/48ae10be-17a8-426b-af57-5124c79aab61/Focus_on_Nonprofit_Employee_Misclassification_slides-06-16-15.pdf

19 De Minimis Fringe Benefits. www.irs.gov/government-entities/federal-state-local-governments/de-minimis-fringe-benefits

20 "Focus on Nonprofit Employee Misclassification" *Venable LLP*

21 IRS Publication 463 Travel, Entertainment, Gift, and Car Expenses www.irs.gov/publications/p463/ch06.html

22 "Hiring Your Workers" *BizFilings,* www.bizfilings.com/toolkit/sbg/office-hr/hiring-workers.aspx

23 "Employers' Responsibility for FICA Payroll Taxes" *BizFilings* www.bizfilings.com/toolkit/sbg/tax-info/payroll-taxes/employers-responsibility-fica-payroll-taxes.aspx

24 "FICA Taxes, Unemployment Insurance, & Workers Comp For Owners," *FitsSmallBusiness,* fitsmallbusiness.com/fica-taxes-unemployment-insurance-and-workers-comp/

25 Instructions for IRS Form 940 Employers Annual Federal Unemployment(FUTA) Tax Return www.irs.gov/pub/irs-pdf/i940.pdf

39548396R00080

Made in the USA
Middletown, DE
18 January 2017